ADVANCE PRAISE FOR *DUMB AND DUMBER*

"The definitive book on the decline of New York and New York City under Andrew Cuomo and Bill de Blasio."

—DAN BONGINO, Host of *The Dan Bongino Show*

"The best book to ever be written by someone else named Matt Palumbo."

—MATT J. PALUMBO, Founder of The Aventine Group

"Matt Palumbo breaks apart the media narrative on New York Governor Andrew Cuomo and New York City Mayor Bill de Blasio's handling of the coronavirus pandemic. Cuomo and de Blasio's actions crippled New York and led to thousands of deaths, while they used the media to craft an image that they were successful in their efforts. Palumbo shows that the only things Cuomo and de Blasio are interested in protecting is their political careers."

—RYAN GIRDUSKY, Author of *They're Not Listening: How The Elites Created The National Populist Revolution*

"Matt has decided to expose us to the truth, that the stars of the progressive movement have little to offer except empty pockets, unsafe cities, and an erosion of common sense. It will be hard to convince anyone who reads this book to stay and suffer in NYC."

—JOE BORELLI, New York City Council Member for the 51st District and Minority Whip of the New York City Council

"As Palumbo so effectively illustrates, New York's greatness cannot be taken for granted. *Dumb and Dumber* lays out in stunning fashion how our nation's largest city, and the state in which it resides, are losing population and wealth on an epic scale thanks to the utter failure of liberal leadership. Palumbo's chronicle of New York's decline is tragic, but critical reading for anyone hoping to grasp an understanding of how a perfect storm of left-wing policy, bloated bureaucracy, and a pandemic is destroying our nation's largest hub—and how it can be saved before it's too late."

—KRISTIN TATE, Author of *The Liberal Invasion of Red State America*

"Matt Palumbo expertly details the sad decline of New York and exposes the hypocrisy and incompetence of two of America's most overrated politicians. Though the story is a sorry one, the failures detailed in this book may reveal remedies for this once-great state and city."

—JACK BUCKBY, Author of *Architects of Betrayal: How Parliament Tried to Thwart Brexit, from Chequers to the Meaningful Vote*

"Matt Palumbo deftly navigates the political terrain of New York City and State in order to expose the malpractice of two of America's worst ever politicians. De Blasio and Cuomo can't hide from the facts, and this book is chock-full of them. Palumbo's impeccable research and eminently readable style expose de Blasio and Cuomo for the incompetent clowns they truly are."

—BARRETT WILSON, Senior Editor at *The Post Millennial*

"It's not just the pandemic that's been deadly for New York—it's the reigns of terror and ineptitude by de Blasio and Cuomo. Palumbo gets to the heart of it in this compelling read about an iconic city in the throes of a steep decline at the behest of these incompetents."

—RAHEEM KASSAM, Host of The National Pulse

Also by Matt Palumbo

Debunk This!: Shattering Liberal Lies

Spygate: The Attempted Sabotage of Donald J. Trump

DUMB AND DUMBER

How Cuomo *and* de Blasio Ruined New York

MATT PALUMBO

A POST HILL PRESS BOOK
ISBN: 978-1-64293-776-3
ISBN (eBook): 978-1-64293-777-0

Dumb and Dumber:
How Cuomo and de Blasio Ruined New York
© 2021 by Matt Palumbo
All Rights Reserved

Cover art by Cody Corcoran

De Blasio Photo by Steve Ferdman/Getty Images
Cuomo Photo by Chip Somodevilla/Getty Images

Post Hill Press
New York • Nashville
posthillpress.com

Published in the United States of America
1 2 3 4 5 6 7 8 9 10

For my parents

TABLE OF CONTENTS

INTRODUCTION

If there's anything nice to be said about Andrew Cuomo and Bill de Blasio, it's how easy they made it to write a short volume on their failures.

There's no shortage of screwups to touch on, but for the sake of this book they're divided into three main categories: coronavirus, economics, and law and order.

The documentation of Cuomo's and de Blasio's response to the coronavirus is the most damning—and a reminder that the mainstream media truly controls the narrative, as you'd have the opposite impression of how New York fared if you only listened to them.

People have been leaving New York for a while now, and just recently NYC began seeing an outflow of population too. A review of the economics of New York, encompassing its high taxation, absurd regulations, inefficient government, and poor social services, leaves no doubt as to why.

And if things couldn't get any worse, the exodus has been catalyzed by the coronavirus and (in NYC in particular) a series of anti-policing policies from de Blasio that are deteriorating law and order and returning his city to what it looked like in its pre–Rudy Giuliani days.

In addition to the sheer incompetence of Cuomo and de Blasio, producing a book on this topic so quickly would not have been possible without the help of a number of others.

Thank you first to Anthony Ziccardi for both presenting me with the opportunity to write such a book and for (accurately) believing that I would be the best person to write it.

Thanks to Katie Sweeney for her phenomenal assistance in helping me research Bill de Blasio's tremulous relationship with the police and his various weak-on-crime policies.

Thanks to The National Pulse's Natalie Winters for her help in piecing together a timeline on de Blasio's and Cuomo's often contradictory statements during their response to the coronavirus pandemic.

Thanks to Kristin Tate, whose great book on why people are leaving blue states, titled *The Liberal Invasion of Red State America*, provided immense guidance in what economic and quality of life indicators to look for when analyzing why people were fleeing New York specifically.

And lastly, thanks to everyone who agreed to read and review this book pre-publication.

Stay tuned for editions two through infinity.

NEW YORK'S CORONAVIRUS DISASTER

To the wrath of countless liberal pundits, President Donald Trump commonly referred to the coronavirus as the "Chinese virus" for the obvious reason that the virus originated in China. Unaware of the many other viruses named after places and people, liberals immediately branded the term "racist" because, let's be honest, it's 2020 and what other argument were you expecting?

While the coronavirus may be the China virus on a global level, in the context of America it's the New York virus. The Empire State quickly became the epicenter of the coronavirus outbreak in the U.S. thanks to the incompetence of Governor Andrew Cuomo and Mayor Bill de Blasio, and from there the virus was exported to the rest of the country.

If New York were its own country, it would have more coronavirus deaths per capita than any other in the entire world as of this writing. At the state level, only New Jersey has more per capita deaths.

But you wouldn't know it if you were fed a steady diet of mainstream media news.

Even as the virus ravaged the state and New York City in particular, the media praised the leadership of the two stooges while condemning Trump. While this would be paradoxical without our media, Andrew Cuomo's approval rating throughout the pandemic surged alongside the virus's death toll in his state.

A review of the media response to the crisis shows Murphy's Law in full effect, hence why the mainstream media is so desperate to ignore it.

DE BLASIO'S ADMINISTRATION DOWNPLAYS A PANDEMIC

NYC's Mayor Bill de Blasio held his first briefing on the looming coronavirus crisis on January 24, a day when his state still had zero confirmed cases. If there was a time to get ahead of the curve to implement preventative measures, this was it. Presented with this opportunity, de Blasio spread disinformation. While acknowledging that the city would eventually be hit by the virus, de Blasio incorrectly assured the public that "what we do know, to date, is that only through prolonged exposure can someone contract this virus. It is not a situation as with some other diseases where a single contact would be enough."

De Blasio's health commissioner, Dr. Oxiris Barbot, was in agreement, stating that "New Yorkers should know the risk to residents of the city is low."

The city's deputy mayor for health and human services, Dr. Raul Perea-Henze, said, "We urge all New Yorkers to continue to pursue their everyday activities and routines, but to remain aware of the facts about coronavirus."[1]

Days later, on January 29, President Donald Trump created his White House Coronavirus Task Force, and then two days after that he restricted entry into the U.S. from China to slow the spread of the virus.

Meanwhile, Health Commissioner Barbot decided that fighting hypothetical racism against Chinese people caused by the virus was more important than fighting the virus itself. "As we gear up to celebrate the Lunar New Year in NYC, I want to assure New Yorkers that there is no reason for anyone to change their holiday plans, avoid the subway, or certain parts of the city because of coronavirus," she tweeted on February 2.[2]

"We're telling New Yorkers, go about your lives, take the subway out, enjoy life," Barbot proclaimed on February 7.[3]

She later stated on the ninth that it was "understandable that people were anxious when there is something new or something

---

1   Jim Geraghty, "The Timeline of How Bill de Blasio Prepared New York City for the Coronavirus," *National Review*, March 27, 2020, https://www.nationalreview.com/2020/03/the-timeline-of-how-bill-de-blasio-prepared-new-york-city-for-the-coronavirus/. ni ma

2   @NYCHealthCommr, "As we gear up to celebrate the #LunarNewYear in NYC, I want to assure New Yorkers that there is no reason for anyone to change their holiday plans, avoid the subway, or certain parts of the city because of #coronavirus," Twitter, February 2, 2020, 12:53 p.m., https://twitter.com/NYCHealthCommr/status/1224043155852537863.

3   Jon Lentz, "New York Political Leaders Who Downplayed the Coronavirus Threat," *City & State*, May 19, 2020, https://www.cityandstateny.com/articles/politics/new-york-state/new-york-political-leaders-who-downplayed-coronavirus-threat.html.

they don't understand and something that may change on a daily basis…. The risk for New Yorkers of the coronavirus is low, and our preparedness as a city is very high. While it is understandable that people feel anxious, that is no way shape or form an excuse for them to use that as an opportunity to spread misinformation, to spread racist ideas because that is currently the greatest risk to New Yorkers."[4]

Dr. Barbot said residents should instead, "come together, know the information and share that information." But she warned, "rumors can be as dangerous as any virus."

Queens state senator John Liu was in agreement, saying that the virus not only caused "unreasonable fears" but that "I've been somewhat disturbed if not outright appalled at some of the comments and gestures that I've seen and my constituents have seen against the Asian community." He asserted that there "is no reason" for anyone to panic or avoid the activities in Chinatown.[5]

On February 10, NYC Council Speaker Corey Johnson tweeted a video of himself in Chinatown celebrating the Lunar New Year. "The Chinese community has been rocked by hateful, xenophobic fears of the coronavirus hurting their businesses. I encourage everyone to #DineInChinatown!" he wrote.[6]

---

4   Todd Maisel, "City Leaders Seek to Allay Fears of Coronavirus in China-town," *AM New York Metro*, February 2, 2020, https://www.amny.com/editorial/city-leaders-seek-to-allay-fears-of-coronavirus-in-chinatown/.

5   Maisel.

6   @NYCSpeakerCoJo, "I was so happy to be in Chinatown yesterday celebrating the #LunarNewYear and eating at some amazing restaurants and bakeries. The Chinese community has been rocked by hateful, xenophobic fears of the coronavirus hurting their businesses. I encourage everyone to #DineInChinatown!" Twitter, February 10 2020, 8:59 p.m., https://twitter.com/NYCSpeakerCoJo/status/1226883517742747648.

The virtue signaling of these officials may have cost lives by encouraging the spread of a virus—but at least they will not be remembered as racist?

"We can really keep this thing contained," de Blasio promised on February 26.

And then came case one.

On March 1, NYC had its first confirmed case, a woman who had just traveled back to New York from Iran. The next day, a man in New Rochelle tested positive even though he hadn't traveled outside the country, indicating that the first confirmed case wasn't the city's actual first case.

Even that did not seem to be a cause for alarm.

"Everybody is doing exactly what we need to do," Governor Cuomo said at a March 2 press conference. "We have been ahead of this from Day 1" (which is an oddly clichéd way of saying "yesterday").

"We'll tell you the second we think you should change your behavior," de Blasio said on March 5.[7] Authorities are "fully prepared to respond," he said. New York City Council Speaker Corey Johnson tweeted that "this is no cause to panic."

"Despite this development, New Yorkers remain at low risk for contracting COVID-19," Barbot chimed in.[8]

They assured the public that the city would begin contacting everyone who was on the flight with the woman who was the

---

7   Chris Francescani, "Timeline: The First 100 Days of New York Gov. Andrew Cuomo's COVID-10 Response," ABC News, June 17, 2020, https://abcnews.go.com/US/News/timeline-100-days-york-gov-andrew-cuomos-covid/story?id=71292880.

8   Tamar Lapin, "NYC Officials: Don't Panic after First Confirmed Coronavirus Case," New York Post, March 1, 2020, https://nypost.com/2020/03/01/nyc-officials-dont-panic-after-first-confirmed-coronavirus-case/.

city's first confirmed case. Dr. Bruce Farber, who is the chief of infectious diseases for the largest hospital system in New York, promised to take action. "Out of an abundance of caution we will be contacting people who were on the flight with her from Iran to New York."

And then, after that, Cuomo and de Blasio never addressed the plane or its passengers ever again—because no one bothered to do the work of tracking down those passengers. Local officials did request an investigation from the Centers for Disease Control and Prevention (CDC), but they didn't perform one because they assumed the woman wasn't contagious.

By March 10, de Blasio was facing calls to shut down the city but said during an appearance on MSNBC's *Morning Joe*: "We cannot shut down because of undue fear. I would advise against these mass closures when we're keeping this situation relatively contained."[9] Because of the exponential growth of viruses, the correct time to scale back human contact is (seemingly paradoxically) when cases are few in order to nip the problem in the bud. Instead, de Blasio decided it would make more sense for the virus to become a massive problem before trying to combat it. Regardless of one's opinion on the merits of lockdowns, the point here is that de Blasio showed no concern about the virus at all, eschewing even basic measures like social distancing and, in fact, encouraging the opposite behavior.

At this time, NYC was relying on fifty disease detectives to trace rising cases across the city. Wuhan, China, had nine thousand such detectives deployed for their city. Near the end

---

9   Julia Marsh, "Coronavirus in NYC: 5 New Cases in City, Bringing Total to 25," *New York Post*, March 10, 2020, https://nypost.com/2020/03/10/coronavirus-in-nyc-5-new-cases-in-city-bringing-total-to-25/.

of March, the Health Department saw fit to finally increase the number of disease detectives—to a meager 150.[10]

On the next day, March 11, de Blasio encouraged people to go on with life as usual, specifically instructing people to dine out at restaurants because the virus "doesn't transmit through food and drink" (it does). "If you're not sick, you should be going about your life," he said. We now know that such advice greatly exacerbated the virus's spread since many people who are infected are either asymptomatic or pre-symptomatic for a period. "If we get to the point where any particular type of activity needs to be suspended, we can do that voluntarily with the organizations or we can mandate it," de Blasio said. "We are doing this day-by-day, hour-by-hour."[11]

He appeared that night on *The Daily Show* with Trevor Noah to joke about elbow bumps.

He later told reporters on March 14: "I am not ready today at this hour to say, let's have a city with no bars, no restaurants, no rec centers, no libraries. I'm not there."[12] It became clear in the following months that de Blasio has no problem swinging between

10   Anna Sanders, "NYC Tripling 'Disease Detectives' to Track Coronavirus among Health Care Workers and Other At-Risk Groups," *Daily News,* March 22, 2020, https://www.nydailynews.com/coronavirus/ ny-coronavirus-disease-detectives-health-care-workers-20200322- fdn4rcw7sjdkdpv4rdf4ga5yay-story.html.

11   Serena Dai, "Mayor Says That Healthy People Should Still Be Dining Out," *Eater,* March 11, 2020, https://ny.eater.com/2020/3/11/21175497/ coronavirus-nyc-restaurants-safe-dine-out.

12   Jake Offenhartz and Christopher Robbins, "With de Blasio's Blessing, NYC Nightlife Still Buzzing Despite Pleas to Self-Isolate," Gothamist, March 15, 2020, https://gothamist.com/news/ pandemic-at-the-disco-nyc-coronavirus-bars.

extremes. Only a few months later, de Blasio would switch to vil- ifying anyone advocating for these same places to reopen.

The unions de Blasio is beholden to eventually led him to close schools. "We understand the immense disruption this will create for our families," United Federation of Teachers presi- dent Michael Mulgrew said. "But right now, more than a million students and staff crisscross the city every day on their way to schools, putting themselves and others at risk of exposure and increasing the likelihood of bringing exposure into their homes and communities."

In hindsight, it now seems that shutting down schools was an overreaction, but de Blasio's motivation for keeping them open in the first place had nothing to do with virology or the fact that the virus barely poses a risk to children. Instead, de Blasio was worried about schools effectively serving as day cares and providers of other city services (such as state-funded school lunches). So, it was by pure accident that he was right about the issue of keeping schools open; the effect of keeping schools open on the transmission of the virus wasn't even on his radar.

De Blasio eventually did shut down the city, and on March 16, after declaring that all gyms must be closed, he foreshadowed the selective enforcement of his policies and got in one final gym run at the Prospect Park YMCA.[13] It wasn't until members of his own staff threatened to resign that de Blasio did so—and regard- less of one's stance on lockdowns, you probably don't want one

---

13   Nate Church, "NYC Mayor Bill de Blasio Ignores Coronavirus Rules to Hit the Gym," Breitbart, March 16, 2020, https://www. breitbart.com/politics/2020/03/16/nyc-mayor-bill-de-blasio-ignores- coronavirus-rules-to-hit-the-gym/.

implemented by someone influenced by staffer temper tantrums over science.

That last gym run predictably produced widespread outrage, including from his own longtime advisors. Advisor Rebecca Katz tweeted that "no current or former staff member should be asked to defend this. The mayor's actions today are inexcusable and reckless." Staffer Jonathan Rosen reacted to Katz's post, "She's right. It's pathetic. Self-involved. Inexcusable." De Blasio later defended himself by saying that he "lives in the regular world"—a defense oddly similar to Alexandria Ocasio-Cortez defending her environmentally destructive behavior while calling for a Green New Deal.

According to former CDC Director and former NYC Health Department Commissioner Tom Frieden, closing schools, non-essential stores, and restaurants two weeks earlier could have reduced the city's mortality by 50–80 percent. "Flu was coming down, and then you saw this new ominous spike. And it was COVID. And it was spreading widely in New York City before anyone knew it," said Frieden. "You have to move really fast. Hours and days. Not weeks. Once it gets a head of steam, there is no way to stop it."[14] While it's impossible to know if such an estimate is true, and many readers are justifiably skeptical of the efficacy of lockdowns, we know for sure that de Blasio did absolutely nothing to get ahead of the virus. And in many cases, his and his colleagues' advice literally encouraged the spread of it.

That would become evident again many times, such as when the debate shifted toward how schools should be reopened. In

---

14   Zack Budryk, "Former CDC Head: New York Death Toll Might Be 80 Percent Lower if Social Distancing Was Enacted 2 Weeks Earlier," The Hill, April 8, 2020, https://thehill.com/homenews/state-watch/491737-former-cdc-head-if-new-york-enacted-social-distancing-2-weeks-earlier.

June, the SOMOS network reached out to de Blasio five times to offer to set up free testing sites to test teachers and schoolchildren. They proposed setting up eighty testing sites, and had 2,500 doctors on staff to conduct tests. De Blasio sat on that offer for two months before replying, and no deal was struck after their initial meeting.[15]

While New York State was the American coronavirus epicenter, within New York, New York City was the epicenter. It was from there that the virus was exported to the rest of the nation, fueling a national crisis.

According to the *New York Times'* summary of the research on the spread of the virus throughout America:

> New York City's coronavirus outbreak grew so large by early March that the city became the primary source of new infections in the United States, new research reveals, as thousands of infected people traveled from the city and seeded outbreaks around the country.
>
> The research indicates that a wave of infections swept from New York City through much of the country before the city began setting social distancing limits to stop the growth. That helped to fuel outbreaks in Louisiana, Texas, Arizona and as far away as the West Coast.
>
> "We now have enough data to feel pretty confident that New York was the primary gateway for the rest of the

---

15 Christopher Cameron, "De Blasio Sat on Offer to Provide Free COVID-19 Testing for Students," *New York Post*, August 29, 2020, https://nypost.com/2020/08/29/de-blasio-sitting-on-offer-of-free-school-covid-19-testing/.

country," said Nathan Grubaugh, an epidemiologist at the Yale School of Public Health.[16]

In total, travel out of New York caused about 65 percent of new coronavirus cases in the U.S. (their report was as of May 7). Nationwide, 92 percent of cases in the Northeast were linked to New York, 82 percent of cases in the South, 78 percent in the Midwest, 78 percent in the West, and 43 percent in the Northwest.

THE DE BLASIO TRAGIC COMEDY OF ERRORS

That the World Health Organization (WHO) and other health leaders gave the world contradictory information has been a common theme in comparing the advice given during the onset of the virus and with the benefit of hindsight. As bad as that was, none of them even come close when it comes to the sheer volume of contradictory and just plain stupid information dispersed by de Blasio.

Virus on Surface

A week after de Blasio's first press conference, he claimed that "we understand some things about this disease" before rattling off a number of falsehoods. "What is clear is the only way you get it is with substantial contact with someone who already has it. You don't get it from a surface. You don't get it from very temporary contact, based on what we know now."

In reality, little was known about the virus's transmissibility on surfaces at the time—but the CDC encouraged people to err

---

16   Benedict Carey and James Glanz, "Travel from New York City Seeded Wave of U.S. Outbreaks," *New York Times*, May 7, 2020, https://www.nytimes.com/2020/05/07/us/new-york-city-coronavirus-outbreak.html.

on the side of caution, warning that it was at least possible that someone could catch the coronavirus by touching a surface and then their mouth, nose, or eyes. De Blasio slightly altered his tune on March 6 to say that the virus could survive on surfaces—but only for two to three minutes. A week later, a study was published proving that the virus could survive on surfaces for days.[17]

In light of the study, de Blasio deflected. "It's not resolved. Our team thinks coronavirus has a very limited shelf life." The CDC, WHO, and even Andrew Cuomo were all stating the opposite by this point.

Asymptomatic Transmission

During his first coronavirus briefing, de Blasio claimed that there was no evidence that casual contact with someone could transmit the virus.

It wasn't until April that de Blasio would tell WNYC's Brian Lehrer that he had realized only in the previous forty-eight hours that asymptomatic individuals could transmit the virus. That was in response to Lehrer pointing out that for months scientists had said asymptomatic transmission was possible.[18]

There is of course mixed evidence on asymptomatic transmission, but it also must be noted that even if asymptomatic individuals weren't capable of spreading the virus, many who have contracted it were *pre*-symptomatic before eventually

---

17   Neeltje van Doremalen et al., "Aerosol and Surface Stability of HCoV-19 (SARS-CoV-2) Compared to SARS-CoV-1," https://www.medrxiv.org/content/10.1101/2020.03.09.20033217v1.full.pdf.

18   Peter Wade, "NYC Mayor Out to Prove That GOP Have Not Cornered the Market on COVID-19 Ignorance," *Rolling Stone,* April 4, 2020, https://www.rollingstone.com/politics/politics-news/nyc-mayor-coronavirus-asymptomatic-statements-978553/.

developing symptoms, and there's no question that they would be able to spread it in that pre-symptomatic period, in addition to the symptomatic period.

Urging People to See Doctors

De Blasio began urging New Yorkers who thought they might have the coronavirus to see a doctor or go to the hospital immediately, which was met with resistance from doctors who didn't have the protective gear or correct equipment to aid such individuals.

It's no secret that infections spread faster in hospitals, and coronavirus is no exception.

De Blasio's health commissioner Dr. Barbot offered different advice, that people should call their doctor first. When asked about the contradictory advice, de Blasio replied that "it's the same thing. It's just a procedural point."

The consequences of de Blasio's advice for frontline health care workers were obvious and immediate. According to a report in the Gothamist:

> On March 7, a hospital in Rockaway saw 41 staffers go into quarantine after an infected patient arrived in the emergency room. The following day, St. John's Episcopal Hospital issued a coronavirus update on its website asking individuals experiencing symptoms to "refrain from visiting."
>
> Two days after the Rockaway patient, more than a week after his own health commissioner clarified the city's

message, de Blasio began instructing people who feel sick to "get on the phone."[19]

What took him so long?

De Blasio Appoints de Blasio

Not deterred by his wife's scandal, where she was unable to account for hundreds of millions of dollars while running the ThriveNYC mental health project, de Blasio appointed First Lady Chirlane McCray as co-chair of the coronavirus "Task Force on Racial Inclusion and Equity." In the words of de Blasio, the purpose of the panel was to address "structural racism that is obviously present in the realities we are facing with this disease"—whatever that means.

The appointment came amid rumors that McCray was planning to run for the presidency of New York's Brooklyn borough, and she certainly wasn't hired for her qualifications in running past projects. In the three years since the founding of the ThriveNYC project headed by McCray, the number of police complaints in the city involving mentally disturbed people increased 23 percent and the number of mentally ill homeless people rose by two thousand.[20] Her Racial Inclusion and Equity task force would accomplish just as little.

A month after McCray's appointment, the city's politicians couldn't help but notice that she accomplished nothing. While

---

19 Elizabeth Kim et al., "The Missteps of Mayor Bill de Blasio's Corona-virus Response," Gothamist, April 6, 2020, https://gothamist.com/news/missteps-mayor-bill-de-blasios-coronavirus-response.

20 Zachary Evans, "Bill de Blasio Appoints Wife as Co-Chair of Coronavirus Racial Inequality Task Force," National Review, April 27, 2020, https://www.nationalreview.com/news/bill-de-blasio-appoints-wife-as-co-chair-of-coronavirus-racial-inequality-task-force/.

the task force had been meeting two to three times per week over video chat, they didn't make a single public statement.

Democratic Brooklyn Councilman Antonio Reynoso complained: "The time for task forces and talk is over. The budget is due in a month, the city is supposed to start reopening in the coming weeks, and all we hear are crickets from City Hall."

"We need real plans and leadership, yet we've heard nothing on how businesses will open safely, how public transit will operate safely, or how the city will begin to reemerge and rebuild," he added. "In the absence of the leadership from the mayor, the City Council is stepping up to lead and help our small businesses and working families get back on their feet."

Staten Island Republican Councilman Joe Borelli asked, "How can we expect urgency on the reopening guidelines we need when there seems to be no urgency on the things the mayor himself is pushing?"[21]

Another Brooklyn Democrat, Councilman Robert Cornegy, also confirmed, "No one's heard anything since the announcement. What [will] happen? We'd have these recommendations and we're going to kick them down the road how far?" The answer turned out to be "indefinitely."

Free Help? Not from Christians

After setting up a field hospital with sixty-eight beds in Central Park in April, Samaritan's Purse learned that it was under investigation for thought crime by the de Blasio administration.

21 Shant Shahrigian, "'The Time for Task Forces Is Over:' NYC Pols Slam Chirlane McCray's Panel on Racial Equity during Coronavirus Crisis," *Daily News*, May 29, 2020, https://www.nydailynews.com/coronavirus/ny-coronavirus-chirlane-mccray-bill-de-blasio-racial-equity-taskforce-20200528-h3w27cup3je4ndbs3ln2252xbm-story.html.

Its "crime" was being a Christian charity led by Franklin Graham. De Blasio cited the group's supposed "homophobia," the bar for which is merely opposing same-sex marriage. Every single Muslim charity would have the exact same belief on the issue of same-sex marriage and homosexuality in general, and de Blasio would be willing to tolerate those beliefs without question.

In response to the news of the Samaritan's Purse hospital, de Blasio said his office would "monitor" the situation because the employees of the charity held a political position the majority of Americans, including Barack Obama, held less than a decade ago.

NYC Council Speaker Corey Johnson expressed concern that Christian medical volunteers would care about the sexuality of those they're volunteering to help (surprise: they don't). "This is very disturbing. We need reassurances from the city and from Mt. Sinai that Samaritan's Purse and its volunteers will be monitored, and that the LGBTQ community will not be discriminated against in any way. This is a crisis, but our values remain," he tweeted out in response to Christians offering his constituents free health care.[22] In other words, if you're a Christian, you're guilty until proven innocent.

State Senator Brad Hoylman of Manhattan, also apparently under the impression that the Samaritan's Purse polls the sexuality of their patients, warned, "Homophobic pastor Franklin Graham and his field hospital operation in Central Park must

---

22   @NYCSpeakerCoJo, "This is very disturbing. We need reassurances from the city and from Mt. Sinai that Samaritan's Purse and its volunteers will be monitored, and that the LGBTQ community will not be discriminated against in any way. This is a crisis, but our values remain," Twitter, March 30, 2020, 6:38 p.m., https://twitter.com/NYCSpeakerCoJo/status/1244771024757043200.

guarantee all LGBTQ patients with COVID-19 are treated with dignity and respect. We'll be watching."[23]

The *National Review*'s Michael Brendan Dougherty illustrated the absurdity of the situation perfectly: "For decades, progressives have been saying: 'Why are Evangelicals so obsessed with sex? Why can't they just do good works and help the needy?' But with New York in crisis, progressives have apparently decided that death would be better than letting disgusting, presumptively-criminal Evangelicals help them."[24]

The small hospital was set up for six weeks and treated 191 patients. Its volunteers didn't receive as much as a "thank-you" from the city for their efforts.

A TALE OF TWO CITIES—NYC VS. SAN FRANCISCO

The failures of de Blasio are best illustrated when his city is compared to another liberal hellhole, San Francisco. New York City is the nation's most densely populated city, while San Francisco is the nation's second most densely populated, so population density cannot explain the wildly different outcomes between the two cities. Inaction in New York City compared to immediate action and preparedness in San Francisco does.

On January 27 San Francisco Mayor London Breed had established an Emergency Operations Center to pair clinicians with emergency responders to identify the city's needs. The

---

23   Nicole Ault, "Christian Relief Comes to Central Park," *Wall Street Journal,* April 5, 2020, https://www.wsj.com/articles/christian-relief-comes-to-central-park-11586111772.

24   Michael Brendan Dougherty, "Evangelicals Are the Real Virus," *National Review,* April 1, 2020, https://www.nationalreview.com/corner/coronavirus-relief-bill-de-blasio-media-criticize-samaritans-purse/.

center figured out where in the city additional hospital beds could be placed and where makeshift hospitals could be built if necessary.

Faced with data showing the virus's ability to overwhelm the city's health care system, Breed issued a local emergency order on February 25.[25] "Although there are still zero confirmed cases in San Francisco residents, the global picture is changing rapidly, and we need to step-up preparedness," Breed said in a statement. "We see the virus spreading in new parts of the world every day, and we are taking the necessary steps to protect San Franciscans from harm." The order didn't yet impose any restrictions on citizens, but aimed to mobilize the city's resources, accelerate emergency planning, and coordinate the otcity's agencies.[26]

Meanwhile, de Blasio held a press conference the next day to reassure the public that everything was A-OK, an attitude he kept throughout March.

On March 2 de Blasio tweeted, "Since I'm encouraging New Yorkers to go on with your lives + get out on the town despite Coronavirus, I thought I would offer some suggestions," before rattling off some ideas for movies to go out and see. In stark contrast, San Francisco's mayor London Breed tweeted on the same day that "we just concluded another public update about the steps we're taking in San Francisco to prepare for the potential

25 London N. Breed, "Fifth Supplement of Mayoral Proclamation Declaring the Existence of a Local Emergency," Office of the Mayor, San Francisco, California, February 25, 2020, https://sfgov.org/olse/sites/default/files/SF_Mayor_Emergency_Declaration_032320_FifthSupplement.pdf.

26 "SF Mayor London Breed Declares Local Emergency Amid Coronavirus Outbreak," NBC Bay Area, February 25, 2020, https://www.nbcbayarea.com/news/local/san-francisco/sf-mayor-london-breed-declared-local-emergency-amid-coronavirus-outbreak/2241796/.

spread of novel coronavirus." She also noted that the city's health department had begun local testing seven days a week.[27]

On March 6, Breed issued an order recommending that people age sixty and older stay home, and encouraged San Francisco employees to eliminate nonessential travel. On March 9, she authorized $5 million in funding to reduce risk of exposure to the homeless. On the day of de Blasio's *The Daily Show* appearance (March 11) gatherings of over a thousand people were banned, and on March 13 that was reduced to one hundred.

It wasn't until March 12 that de Blasio issued an emergency order, once his city had ninety-five confirmed cases.

On March 16, five days after de Blasio's appearance on *The Daily Show*, San Francisco's Mayor issued a shelter-in-place order (and schools were already closed). On that day, San Francisco had a total of forty patients confirmed to have coronavirus, while NYC had 463.[28]

By the end of May, San Francisco had 7,746 tests per 100,000 residents, 291 positive cases per 100,000 residents, and five deaths per 100,000 residents. In stark contrast, NYC had 11,745 tests per 100,000 residents, 2,409 positive cases per 100,000 residents, and an incredible 258 deaths per 100,000 residents.[29] By the begin-

---

27   Amy Graff, "Tweets Show SF and NYC Mayors' Drastically Different Approaches to Outbreak," *San Francisco Gate,* April 9, 2020, https://www.sfgate.com/bayarea/article/de-Blasio-London-Breed-tweets-coronavirus-March-2-15189898.php#photo-19278576.

28   Elizabeth Kim et al., "The Missteps of Mayor Bill de Blasio's Coronavirus Response," Gothamist, April 6, 2020, https://gothamist.com/news/missteps-mayor-bill-de-blasios-coronavirus-response.

29   Beth Daley, "Coronavirus Deaths in San Francisco vs. New York: What Causes Such Big Differences in Cities' Tolls?" The Conversation, June 2, 2020, https://theconversation.com/coronavirus-deaths-in-san-francisco-vs-new-york-what-causes-such-big-differences-in-cities-tolls-138399.

ning of August, San Francisco only had 64 deaths and 7,000 cases out of a population of over 800,000 (still about 5 deaths per 100,000 people).[30]

When asked by CNN about his prior comments urging New Yorkers to go about their lives, de Blasio responded that "we should not be focusing, in my view, on anything looking back on any level of government right now."[31] In other words, there's "nothing to see here."

New York's excess deaths came despite the citizens of the state doing everything correctly themselves. It's ironic in a tragic sense that New York's citizens were statistically among the most responsible in how they reacted to the virus, yet suffered the highest per capita death toll.

Fifty-three percent of New Yorkers wore masks in public, while 30 percent stayed home when possible. The state was also best positioned to fight the virus with 373 physicians for every 100,000 residents and only 6.6 percent of people uninsured.[32]

So who else is there to blame but their leaders?

NYC Health Commissioner Resigns

Dr. Barbot would later resign on August 4, citing de Blasio's incompetence in her resignation letter. "I leave my post today

---

30 Christina Farr, "How San Francisco Succeeded More Than Other U.S. Cities in Fighting the Coronavirus." CNBC, August 8, 2020, https://www.cnbc.com/2020/08/08/how-san-francisco-beat-other-us-cities-in-fighting-the-coronavirus.html.

31 Jacob Knutson, "De Blasio on Downplaying Crisis: 'None of Us Have Time to Look Backward," Axios, March 29, 2020, https://www.axios.com/new-york-city-de-blasio-coronavirus-comments-34cf5a9b-9b5d-4987-97d6-e9fd3ba03e24.html.

32 D. Gilson, "Coronavirus & Responsible Behaviors by State [+Insurance Advice]," The Truth About Insurance, July 16, 2020, https://www.thetruthaboutinsurance.com/coronavirus-responsible-behaviors-by-state/.

with deep disappointment that during the most critical public health crisis in our lifetime, that the Health Department's incomparable disease control expertise was not used to the degree it could have been," she wrote.

But she wasn't without her own scandals that fueled the spread of the virus.

In May, Barbot ignored a request from the NYPD requesting hundreds of thousands of surgical masks and reportedly told a high-ranking police official that she doesn't "give two rats' asses about your cops. I need them for others." She'd later publicly apologize after de Blasio called on her to apologize.[33] That was after there was a clear demand for them—by just the second week of April, over one-fifth of the entire NYPD were out sick.[34]

NEW YORK—A TALE OF TWO CAUTIONARY TALES

As mentioned previously, if New York were its own country, it would rank number one in the entire world in terms of coronavirus deaths per capita. (This title is also true of New Jersey, which is the only state with more deaths per capita than New York.)

Sweden has been the go-to country in arguments over the legitimacy of lockdowns in fighting the coronavirus. Sweden

---

33 Sydney Kashiwagi, "Health Commissioner Apologizes to NYPD for 'I Don't Give Two Rats' Asses about Your Cops' Remark," *Staten Island Advance*, May 18, 2020, https://www.silive.com/coronavirus/2020/05/health-commissioner-apologizes-to-nypd-for-i-dont-give-two-rats-asses-about-your-cops-remark.html.

34 Craig McCarthy and Julia Marsh, "Huge Percentage of NYPD Cops Out Sick as Coronavirus Spreads," *New York Post,* April 6, 2020, https://nypost.com/2020/04/06/nearly-20-percent-of-nypd-cops-are-out-sick-during-coronavirus-outbreak/.

notably never had a national lockdown, and the results thereafter have become a sort of Rorschach test for pro- and anti-lockdown individuals.

The case against Sweden's approach is easy to see when compared against the rest of the Nordic countries—i.e., those most similar to them demographically. On a per capita basis, Sweden had roughly ten times the total deaths of its neighbors. Of course, it is entirely possible that when you factor in consequences of lockdowns such as increased suicides and drug overdoses, the gap in deaths is much smaller. It's also of note that in the half-decade preceding the pandemic, Sweden had far fewer flu deaths than the rest of Scandinavia, meaning that there was a higher population of elderly people who were now killed by the coronavirus instead.[35]

The *New York Times* warned in a headline that "Sweden Has Become the World's Cautionary Tale" in an article dated July 7. Meanwhile when it came to Cuomo and his nursing home disaster, the *Times* reported as if it was a political debate. "What went wrong? The effort to answer that question has become politically charged, with Republican lawmakers using the deaths to try to undermine Gov. Andrew M. Cuomo, a third-term Democrat," the article read.[36]

---

35 Joakim Book, Christian Bjørnskov, and Daniel B. Klein, "Sweden's High Covid Death Rates Among the Nordics: 'Dry Tinder' and Other Important Factors," American Institute for Economic Research, August 29, 2020, https://www.aier.org/article/swedens-high-covid-death-rates-among-the-nordics-dry-tinder-and-other-important-factors/.

36 Joseph A. Wulfsohn, "*New York Times* Accused of Going Soft on Cuomo over NY Nursing Home Controversy," Fox News, July 9, 2020, https://www.foxnews.com/media/new-york-times-accused-of-going-soft-on-cuomo-over-ny-nursing-home-controversy.

In a press conference, Cuomo dismissed Sweden's herd immunity strategy as one where "a lot of people die."[37]

But ironically, you'd have been safer living in Sweden than New York during the height of the pandemic, and overall.

While daily deaths in Sweden peaked at around ten per million people, they approached forty per million people per day in New York.[38]

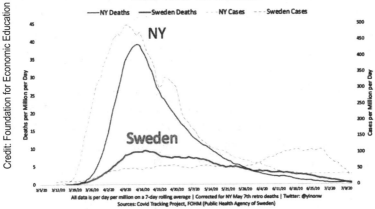

Deaths (Solid Lines) and Cases (Dotted Lines) New York vs. Sweden

By mid-July, when Sweden and NY saw their daily death tolls finally approach zero, New York had 1,670 coronavirus deaths

---

37   "Cuomo Acknowledges Sweden's Herd Immunity Strategy," C-Span, April 22, 2020, www.c-span.org/video/?c4872436%2Fuser-clip-cuomo-acknowledges-swedens-herd-immunity-strategy.

38   Jon Miltimore, "Why Sweden Succeeded in "Flattening the Curve" and New York Failed," Foundation for Economic Education, July 15, 2020, https://fee.org/articles/why-sweden-succeeded-in-flattening-the-curve-and-new-york-failed/.

per million people,[39] New York City had nearly 2,000, while Sweden had 549.[40] For reference, the rate for the U.S. as a whole at the time was 422 per million, but that figure is heightened due to New York bringing up the average.

ANDREW CUOMO'S FATAL NURSING HOME ORDER

At the center of New York's coronavirus disaster was the entirely preventable decision to treat coronavirus patients in nursing homes. We know now that it's predominantly the elderly and those with preexisting conditions whose lives are threatened by the virus, and any strategy to fight the damage caused by the virus must focus on protecting them. New York did the opposite.

Kicking off Andrew Cuomo's litany of errors is his now infamous "March 25 advisory" issued to nursing home administrators, directors of nursing, and hospital discharge planners.[41]

The supposed logic behind the order was that it would help free up space in the hospitals for seriously ill coronavirus patients (while those less severely affected by the virus could recover in other long-term care facilities, primarily nursing homes).

The order states (emphasis theirs): *"No resident shall be denied re-admission or admission to the nursing home solely based on a confirmed or suspected diagnosis of COVID-19. Nursing homes*

---

39 John Elflein, "COVID-19 Death Rates in the United States as of August 7, 2020, by State," Statista, August 7, 2020, https://www.statista.com/statistics/1109011/coronavirus-covid19-death-rates-us-by-state/.

40 Raynor de Best, "COVID-19 Deaths Worldwide Per One Million Population as of August 7, 2020, by Country," Statista, August 7, 2020, https://www.statista.com/statistics/1104709/coronavirus-deaths-worldwide-per-million-inhabitants/.

41 New York Department of Health, "Advisory: Hospital Discharges and Admission to Nursing Homes," March 25, 2020, http://www.hurlbutcare.com/images/NYSDOH_Notice.pdf.

are prohibited from requiring a hospitalized resident who is determined medically stable to be tested for COVID-19 prior to admission or readmission."

The order put nursing homes in the position where they'd be forced to treat those infected with coronavirus. With that fact alone, one can immediately see how such a policy would cause mass death. While a sane individual would prioritize the safety of the elderly against a virus that disproportionately kills the elderly, logic was lost on the Cuomo administration (who would later attempt to blame this all on Trump's CDC—but more on that defense later).

The rules were simple: if a hospital determined that a patient who needed a nursing home was stable, the home had no choice but to take them. Making matters worse, New York was the only state in the union that barred testing of those being placed in or returning to nursing homes, so it was impossible to know if someone was newly infected or otherwise still contagious. As many as 4,500 patients infected with coronavirus were sent to nursing homes.

What could possibly go wrong? Everything.

As ProPublica notes in its June 16 report excoriating Cuomo's policy:

> In the weeks that followed the March 25 order, COVID-19 tore through New York state's nursing facilities, killing more than 6,000 people—about 6% of its more than 100,000 nursing home residents.
>
> States that issued orders similar to Cuomo's recorded comparably grim outcomes. Michigan lost 5% of roughly 38,000 nursing home residents to COVID-19 since the

outbreak began. New Jersey lost 12% of its more than 43,000 residents.

In Florida, where such transfers were barred, just 1.6% of 73,000 nursing home residents died of the virus. California, after initially moving toward a policy like New York's, quickly revised it. So far, it has lost 2% of its 103,000 nursing home residents.[42]

Meanwhile, the Republican county executive of Rensselaer County rightly saw Cuomo's advice as absurd and defied it. The only nursing home run by the county, Van Rensselaer, saw a total of zero coronavirus deaths.

Cuomo Plays Defense

After roughly six thousand of New York's nursing home residents had died, Cuomo was asked on May 20 about calls for a federal probe into the state's handling of the coronavirus. At the center of the calls for inquiry was the March advisory that caused the state to handle nursing homes in the least sane way possible.

In character for a Democrat in the modern era, Cuomo took the default position of blaming President Donald Trump for his mess. "Anyone who wants to ask why the state did that with COVID patients in nursing homes, it's because the state followed

---

42 Joaquin Sapien and Joe Sexton, "'Fire Through Dry Grass': Andrew Cuomo Saw COVID-19's Threat to Nursing Homes. Then He Risked Adding to It," ProPublica, June 16, 2020, https://www.propublica.org/article/fire-through-dry-grass-andrew-cuomo-saw-covid-19-threat-to-nursing-homes-then-he-risked-adding-to-it.

President Trump's CDC's guidance," Cuomo said. "So they should ask President Trump."[43]

It should be noted that nearly all the states that had similarly disastrous nursing home policies were run by Democrats, so it would certainly be odd for only Democrat leaders to heed the advice of Trump's CDC and then turn around and blame Trump for taking his advice.

Regardless, there's no need to "ask President Trump" anything. Cuomo's defense is a lie he knows he can get away with because no one in the media will fact-check him on it.

Cuomo's Defense Falls Apart

In the CDC's guidance Cuomo is referencing, issued two days before his March 25 order, the CDC cited two key factors to determine if a patient with coronavirus should be discharged to a nursing home. Those factors were if the patient was medically ready for the discharge and if the nursing home could safely care for an infected patient by implementing all recommended protocols to stop the spread of the virus.

That wasn't the only guidance issued, either. The CDC's Morbidity and Mortality Report was released a week earlier and also stressed that "in the context of rapidly escalating COVID-19 outbreaks in much of the United States, it is critical that long-term care facilities implement active measures to prevent introduction of COVID-19."

The U.S. Centers for Medicare and Medicaid Services (CMS), which is the federal regulator of nursing homes, also issued guidance—and says that Cuomo didn't follow it. The top CMS

---

43   Nick Reisman, "Defending Nursing Home Policy, Cuomo Points to CDC's Guidelines," State of Politics, May 20, 2020, https://nystateofpolitics. com/state-of-politics/new-york/ny-state-of-politics/2020/05/20/ defending-nursing-home-policy--cuomo-points-to-cdc-s-guidelines.

administrator made it clear that nursing homes were only to accept those patients for which they could provide care (as per guidance the CMS issued on March 13). They would later say a week after Cuomo's order that new long-term care patients should be screened for coronavirus testing "if available." CMS guidance also stated that nursing homes should dedicate a specific wing exclusively to returning residents to quarantine for fourteen days.

And Cuomo's guidance didn't allow for that. As PolitiFact notes:

> …Once the state issued its March 25 advisory, nursing home operators said that they felt they had no choice but to accept residents who were either known to be infected or suspected to be. *That's because the March 25 memo did not say anything about making sure that a nursing home can care for a patient before making an admission decision, and said they "must comply with the expedited receipt of residents."* In the month following the memo, nursing homes pleaded for relief from the order.[44]

Furthermore, as ProPublica notes in its analysis, "New York was the only state in the nation that barred testing of those being placed or returning to nursing homes."

It's for reasons like these that The Society for Post-Acute and Long-Term Care Medicine (AMDA) issued a statement on March 26 opposing the order: "We find the New York State

---

44 Jill Terreri Ramos, "New York's Nursing Home Policy Was Not Fully in Line with CDC," PolitiFact, June 13, 2020, https://www.politifact.com/factchecks/2020/jun/13/andrew-cuomo/new-yorks-nursing-home-policy-was-not-line-cdc/.

Advisory to be over-reaching, not consistent with science, unenforceable, and beyond all, not in the least consistent with patient safety principles."

Those concerns were reiterated three days later in a joint statement by AMDA, American Health Care Association, and National Center for Assisted Living.[45]

Undeterred by common sense, on April 23 Cuomo told nursing homes that they "don't have the right to object" to the state's policy.

It wasn't until May 10 that Cuomo issued an executive order that state hospitals "shall not discharge a patient to a nursing home, unless the nursing home operator or administrator has first certified that it is able to properly care for such a patient." The order also requires that a patient must be tested for COVID-19, and the test must be negative.

It took him long enough.

The nursing home order was unquestionably a disaster and, in an admission of defeat, it has since been scrubbed from the state's website.

Cuomo Plays Defense—Round 2.0

As if the initial defense Cuomo tried to muster wasn't unconvincing enough, the New York Health Department issued its own report on July 6 to assure the public that the New York Health

---

45 The Society for Post-Acute and Long-term Care Medicine, "State Advisories re: Hospital Discharges and Admissions to Nursing Homes and Assisted Living Communities," March 29, 2020, http://paltc.org/sites/default/files/AMDA-AHCA-NCAL%20Statement%20on%20State%20Advisories%20FINAL.pdf.

Department did nothing wrong. After all, the New York Health Department said so.[46]

One New York state assemblyman, Democrat Ron Kim, rightly slammed the report as a cover-up, and pointed out the obvious conflict of interest in having the health department investigate itself. Who was expecting the report to admit any failures?

According to the New York Health Department report:

> According to data submitted by nursing homes, in many cases under the penalty of perjury, approximately 37,500 nursing home staff members—one in four of the state's approximately 158,000 nursing home workers—were infected with COVID-19 between March and early June 2020. Of the 37,500 nursing home staff infected, nearly 7,000 of them were working in facilities in the month of March; during the same period, more than a third of the state's nursing home facilities had residents ill with the virus. Roughly 20,000 infected nursing home workers were known to be COVID-positive by the end of the month of April. These workforce infections are reflective of the larger geographic impact of the virus's presence across the state.

The problem with putting blame on nursing home workers rather than the infected patients they treated is ridiculous for two reasons. First, as already documented, nursing homes were barred from testing those entering their facilities. Second, Patrice Adeline, an RN who volunteered for three weeks at a Queens

---

46 New York Department of Health, "New York State Department of Health Issues Report on COVID-19 in Nursing Homes," 2020, www.health.ny.gov/press/releases/2020/2020-07-06_covid19_nursing_home_report.htm.

nursing home, told me that staff was tested before every shift. "Staff had their temps checked upon entering the building and tested for COVID so no one ever worked with symptoms and the new data shows that transmitting the virus is unlikely if you're not showing symptoms." In other words, staff could have only been responsible for getting others sick if they happened to receive false negatives on their daily testing.

It's more likely the case that NY's health department is getting correlation backwards—that it was staff that were also infected by patients. "The problem was Cuomo's direction to put sick people next to healthy people. I mean the floor I was on was all healthy and then in two weeks' time half the floor got sick," Adeline told me.

Not coincidentally, the New York State Nurses Association has sued the Health Department and its commission for failing to adequately equip frontline medical workers with protective wear and for allowing hospitals to order nurses sickened by the virus back to work.

So what's the Health Department's justification for why it's not responsible for its actions?

The report claims, "The data does not show a consistent relationship between admissions and increased mortality...there were cases where nursing homes did not admit any COVID-positive patients, yet still had a high number of COVID-related deaths." This is a particularly insane line of reasoning, because as already documented, they did not test patients entering their facilities.

Perhaps among the homes that did accept patients from hospitals there were some that somehow avoided any coronavirus patients by pure chance, but rather than deal in hypotheticals, we already know that one nursing home didn't comply with NY's order, and it was the sole nursing home with no coronavirus deaths. If we're to believe that 81 percent of nursing homes had infected staff, either this one nursing home was in the fortunate 19 percent, or there's more at play.

Indeed, if the nursing home policy wasn't an unmitigated disaster, Cuomo wouldn't have needed to make excuses for why it was Trump's fault, nor would the policy have been repealed. He also wouldn't have needed his health department to cover it all up.

The New York State Nurses Association wasn't buying it either and called for an independent review of the nursing home situation. "New Yorkers deserve a full accounting of what happened over the past four months and the NYSDOH nursing home report, unfortunately, does not move us forward. The need is plain for a comprehensive, independent review of nursing home practices, the role of for-profit operations, and NYSDOH oversight."[47]

As absurd as it is having a government agency effectively investigate itself, that's just the tip of the iceberg when it comes to the conflicts of interest present.

Buried in a footnote in the report is that McKinsey & Company analyzed the data for the nursing home study. Previously, the Cuomo administration had relied on projections from McKinsey that New York would need 55,000–110,000 hospital beds and 25,000–37,000 ventilators. Those projections fortunately turned out to be massively overstated—but at the time they were what

---

47   "Statement from the New York State Nurses Association on NYS Department of Health Report on Nursing Home Covid-19 Deaths," New York State Nurses Association, July 9, 2020, https://www.nysna. org/press/2020/statement-new-york-state-nurses-association-nys-department-health-report-nursing-home#.XwyvhyhKiUk.

led to the disastrous nursing home policy in order to free up hospital beds.[48]

So not only did the New York Department of Health produce a study exonerating the New York Department of Health, it was aided by McKinsey to analyze the data regarding the policies its shoddy projections had spawned. Seldom does a study's conflict of interest itself have a conflict of interest.

The True Nursing Home Death Toll Remains Unknown

While the Cuomo administration invested in covering up its nursing home scandal, it has not put any effort toward uncovering what the nursing home death toll truly is. It is no surprise that it is putting optics over truth.

When it comes to the true nursing home death toll, New York Health Commissioner Howard Zucker does not have an answer. Upon being pressed about it by the New York State Assembly and Senate at a hearing, he said he would "get back" to them (which is a polite way of saying that he won't get back to them).

Zucker left the hearing before those impacted by the order were set to testify. One painted a harrowing picture of how New York handled the crisis:

My belief is the following: My mother died because she was starved. My mother died of dehydration. My mother died because of lack of PPE, therefore, the staff never entered her room to provide care for fear of getting infected. My mother died of COVID-19 although she was never tested so precautions were not taken. My mother died of COVID-19 because residents

---

48 Chuck Ross, "Andrew Cuomo's Report on Nursing Home Deaths Marked by Clear Conflicts of Interest," Daily Caller, June 12, 2020, https://dailycaller.com/2020/07/12/andrew-cuomo-new-york-nursing-home-deaths-coronavirus-mckinsey/.

[were] not properly isolated. My mother died because proper infection-control protocols were not followed. My mother died because the nursing home accepted positive patients from the hospitals as per Governor Cuomo. My mother died alone, isolated from her family and drowning in abject misery. According to Governor Cuomo, coronavirus in a nursing home was like "fire through dry grass" and that the seniors were his top priority. He lied. He let our seniors die. He let my mother die along with 100 of her peers at Isabella. There was no obligation for Isabella Geriatric Center to maintain a high or even standard level of care, to retain proper staffing levels, to retain proper medical records, to provide adequate personal protective equipment, and to keep up with proper infection-control protocols. Immunity given to the nursing homes by Governor Cuomo resulted in the deaths of thousands of precious lives in New York State.[49]

Another witness commented that "an external investigation should be done as to why State would accept this, as they've [accepted] so much of the abhorrent maltreatment to patients. Covid related infections and death numbers noted by New York State from any hospital or nursing home or health assisted facility are obviously higher. Much higher. I'm hearing from authorities they're thinking close to 20,000."

It may not be twenty thousand higher, but there's strong evidence that true nursing home deaths could be more than double the reported number.

---

49   Cortney O'Brien, "Witnesses Convinced That Cuomo Is Intentionally Hiding Actual Number of Nursing Home Deaths," *Townhall,* August 5, 2020, https://townhall.com/tipsheet/cortneyobrien/2020/08/05/ witnesses-convinced-that-cuomo-is-intentionally-hiding-actual-number-of-nursing-homes-deaths-n2573668.

An Associated Press report noted that New York is the only state that only counts residents who died on nursing home property from coronavirus and not those who were transported to hospitals and died there as nursing home deaths. In other states, nursing home resident deaths make up 44 percent of total coronavirus nursing home deaths, which would imply an additional eleven thousand nursing home deaths in New York if that percent holds constant (and in reality, it's probably larger).[50]

When the Empire Center filed a Freedom of Information Law request seeking a count on nursing home deaths, including how many had died after being transferred to hospitals before dying, it was told by the Health Department that they couldn't find the records.[51]

In response to all the concern over the true number of nursing home deaths, Cuomo laughably claims that there's no need for any independent investigation into that—and says that you'd "have to be blind" not to think calls for such an investigation are anything but political.[52]

The tens of thousands who lost family and friends disagree and deserve to know what the logic behind his nursing home

50 Bernard Condon, Matt Sedensky, and Meghan Hoyer, "New York's True Nursing Home Death Toll Cloaked in Secrecy," Associated Press, August 11, 2012, https://apnews.com/212ccd87924b690 6053703a00514647f.

51 Bill Hammond, "The Health Department Stalls a FOIL Request for the Full COVID Death Toll in Nursing Homes," Empire Center, September 1, 2020, https://www.empirecenter.org/publications/the-health-department-stalls-a-foil/.

52 Brooke Singman, "Cuomo Rejects Independent Investigation of Nursing Home Coronavirus Deaths as Political," Fox News, August 10, 2020, https://www.foxnews.com/politics/cuomo-coronavirus-nursing-home-independent-investigation.

decision was, when Cuomo himself said that even he wouldn't put his mother in a nursing home in a time like this.[53]

Cuomo's Pandemic Preparedness

One common claim spread by the media is that the Obama administration left a pandemic playbook for the Trump administration to follow, which it shredded. It created the impression that the administration went in blind when combating the pandemic, when in reality the Obama plan was replaced by two other pandemic response reports.

The Trump administration conducted the Crimson Contagion 2019 Functional Exercise, which tested the capacity of the federal government and twelve states to response to an influenza pandemic originating specifically from China. The Department of Health and Human Services (HHS) issued a report on the exercise in January 2020, which criticizes Obama's playbook because it "does not provide the requisite mechanisms or processes to effectively lead the coordination of the federal government's response."

Cuomo too had a pandemic playbook, which was created in 2006 and ran hundreds of pages in length. The document was called the "Pandemic Influenza Response Plan" and was most recently updated in 2014. The document warned about such a pandemic's ability to overwhelm New York's health care system and highlighted the need for a large stockpile of emergency equipment and protective gear, and a way to expand the number of hospital beds available.

---

53   Lindsey Ellefson, "Gov Cuomo Says He Wouldn't Put His Own Mother in a Nursing Home Right Now," Yahoo Entertainment, May 27, 2020, https://www.yahoo.com/entertainment/gov-cuomo-says-wouldn-t-203014271.html.

New York didn't have the former. One senior health executive recalled Cuomo asking of the state's stockpile, "What's in it? Is it expired?" It wasn't until March 16 that Cuomo created a task force to expand the number of hospital beds—something the CEO of the largest hospital organization in the state (Northwell Health) said should have been done a month earlier.

That CEO, Michael Dowling, said he didn't even know the document existed, and commented that "a plan on a piece of paper that doesn't have an operational part means nothing."

ProPublica asked the New York Health Department spokesman if hospitals statewide were aware of the plan, and he responded that "representatives from all responding services to the multi-service plan meet several times throughout the year to review and update the plan."

New York's stockpile was created around the time the 2006 plan was issued—and when the coronavirus hit, it was brought to light that five years prior, the de Blasio administration had auctioned off hundreds of city-owned ventilators due to the cost of maintaining them. The 2006 report acknowledged that "since the pandemic will be widespread in the United States, the supplies from the federal Strategic National Stockpile may not be available and local caches will need to be relied upon."

That proved prophetic. De Blasio warned on May 3 that NYC would run out of its current supply of ventilators by Monday or Tuesday of the subsequent week,[54] while Cuomo had warned a day earlier that the state would run out of its stockpile within six days without assistance. The next month, Cuomo would per-

---

54 Marty Johnson, "De Blasio: NYC Can 'Only Get to Monday or Tuesday' with Current Ventilator Supply," The Hill, April 3, 2020, https://thehill. com/homenews/state-watch/490982-de-blasio-nyc-can-only-get-to-monday-or-tuesday-with-current-ventilators.

sonally thank China for delivering one thousand ventilators to New York.[55]

New York would also pay $69 million for 1,450 ventilators it never received after taking up an offer of help from a Twitter user with the screen name "Yopines" who had 128 followers at the time of his offer.[56]

The pandemic plan also called for the mass distribution of masks to the public—something else that never happened.

New York's Bureaucratic Nightmare

To prevent overcrowding, New York opted for a disastrous nursing home policy, the consequences of which were obvious to anyone except them.

All hospitals were strained due to the pandemic, but public facilities more than private. Where a typical emergency room has roughly four patients per nurse, government hospitals in New York had ten to fifteen patients per nurse (and sometimes twenty). For private facilities, the ratio was six to seven patients per nurse. One doctor at a government hospital told the *New York Times* that roughly 20–30 percent of deaths he saw could have been prevented had patients been properly treated.[57]

---

55 Jennifer Peltz, Amy Forliti, and David Rising (Associated Press), "New York Gets Chinese Ventilators; Trump Wants More Thanks," *U.S. News*, April 4, 2020, https://www.usnews.com/news/world/articles/2020-04-04/competition-for-supplies-sharpening-as-pandemic-worsens.

56 Stephanie Pagones, "New York Spent $69 Million on Ventilators That Never Arrived: Report," Fox Business, April 30, 2020, https://www.foxbusiness.com/healthcare/new-york-coronavirus-ventilators-trump-twitter.

57 Hannah Cox, "New York's Failure to Use Emergency Hospitals Is Another Reason to Distrust Government Healthcare," *Washington Examiner*, August 3, 2020, https://www.washingtonexaminer.com/opinion/new-yorks-failure-to-use-emergency-hospitals-is-another-reason-to-distrust-government-healthcare.

The city's coronavirus mortality rate was as much as three times higher in public hospitals than private.

Compounding the matter, public hospitals had exclusive agreements with ambulance providers requiring them to take people to their overcrowded hospitals.

Meanwhile, to expand capacity, New York City started building makeshift hospitals, which were seldom used. (No word on if there was a religious test for those who built them.) One hospital built at the Billie Jean King National Tennis Center had 470 beds, and only saw seventy-nine patients before closing.

That wasn't due to a lack of demand for those hospitals like many concluded; it was because a labyrinth of red tape made it impossible to utilize them. As Hannah Cox explained in the *Washington Examiner*:

> There were multiple problems here. First, doctors were forced into a spiderweb of red tape upon arrival. They were given ridiculous amounts of paperwork, orientations, and training on computers, tying up their time during the height of the disease. Secondly, city officials went back and forth on the criteria for who could be admitted to the overflow hospitals and gave conflicting data to providers on which patients to transfer. They landed on 25 exclusionary criteria that blocked patients, with symptoms such as fever from being moved. A fever is, of course, one of the primary symptoms of COVID-19. They also implemented rules that blocked the admittance of patients with symptoms deemed not severe enough. This resulted in many COVID-19 patients quarantining and dying in hotel rooms without access to care.[58]

---

58   Cox.

To borrow the Cato Institute's description, a similar "red tape epidemic" could be seen when President Trump sent the USNS *Comfort* to take patients, which never saw more than 179 patients.

The USNS *Comfort* arrived in New York harbor on March 30 with 1,000 hospital beds and 1,200 staff to treat *non*-coronavirus patients and to relieve the brunt of the burden from hospitals.

Due to regulations, patients couldn't be admitted directly to the ship, and ambulances weren't allowed to take people to them. Patients had to be evaluated in a regular hospital first before being transferred to the ship. There was a list of forty-nine medical conditions for which patients had to be screened before being admitted, and patients needed a negative coronavirus test (a requirement removed days later).

On the ship's first day in operation, twenty patients were tested, and things didn't get much better from there.

On April 6, Cuomo changed course, and sought and was granted permission from President Trump to let the ship take coronavirus patients. The ship was then reconfigured into a 500-bed hospital. That same day, a crew member tested positive for the virus despite the crew having been ordered to quarantine for two weeks prior to their trek to New York.

And then nothing happened. According to a report published in the *New York Post*, Cobble Hill Health Center's CEO Donny Tuchman sent a series of desperate emails to Health Department officials on April 9, notifying them that a Brooklyn nursing home, where fifty-five patients ultimately died of coronavirus, was overwhelmed. Tuchman asked for permission to send his suspected coronavirus patients to either the Javits Convention Center makeshift hospital or to the USNS *Comfort*. At the time of the email, the Javits Center had 886 free beds, and the *Comfort* had 438.

He was denied.

By April 21, the ship had only treated 179 patients, and that was all they'd treat.

Cuomo to Out-of-State Health Care Workers: Thanks— but Not That Much

Throughout the pandemic, over eighty thousand out-of-state health care workers headed to New York to help.

Cuomo was so "appreciative" of them that he decided to keep the double-taxation his state applies to the income they earned. Not only would they have to pay income tax on their income at the rate of whatever their home state is, they'd have to pay New York's, which ranges from 5 percent to 8.82 percent.

"We're not in a position to provide any subsidies right now because we have a $13 billion deficit," Cuomo said, referring to not taxing medical workers as subsidizing them, even though a subsidy is the opposite of a tax.

"So there's a lot of good things I'd like to do, and if we get federal funding, we can do, but it would be irresponsible for me to sit here looking at a $13 billion deficit and say I'm gonna spend more money, when I can't even pay the essential services."[59] Cuomo would later come out against raising taxes on the wealthy to plug the budget gap.

And that wasn't all. According to *Forbes*'s Patrick Gleason:

New York State and local governments received more than $7.5 billion in pandemic relief funding through

---

59   Patrick Gleason, "Andrew Cuomo Confirms New York Will Tax Out-of-State Volunteer Health Workers. Congress Can Stop This," *Forbes*, May 8, 2020, https://www.forbes.com/sites/patrickgleason/2020/05/08/andrew-cuomo-confirms-new-york-will-tax-out-of-state-volunteer-health-workers-congress-can-stop-this/#4354e0c75f12.

the CARES Act approved with bipartisan congressional support in March. Governor Cuomo is now demanding more money and apparently sees out-of-state volunteer health workers as [a] bargaining chip. Samaritan's Purse, the non-profit that erected and staffed a temporary hospital in Central Park, was shocked to discover that they would be getting an income tax bill from Albany.

As you'll glean from the economics section of this book, this is all in character for a state that taxes anything with a pulse (and in some cases, even without a pulse).

THE PROTESTS

At the end of May and the beginning of June, politicians and the media helped spawn what must have been the fastest narrative shift in media and political history. While just days prior, anyone who wanted so much as a haircut (or to open their business because their livelihood was destroyed) went from being labeled a selfish "grandma killer" to a racist if they weren't out in the streets protesting for Black Lives Matter.

De Blasio told protesters that despite us being in the middle of a pandemic, they were encouraged to protest peacefully. "To all the people who are protesting—please, even if you are expressing that pain, that anger, that sense that something is wrong, and must be fixed—please remember how important it is to protest peacefully. Remember the only way were gonna make things right is by somehow finding a way to work together."[60]

---

60 Luis Diaz, "Mayor de Blasio: 'If You Are Angry...Direct That Anger to All of Us,'" *New Yorkled Magazine,* May 29, 2020, https://www.newyorkled. com/mayor-de-blasio-if-you-are-angry-direct-that-anger-to-all-of-us/.

In defense of his own hypocrisy, de Blasio said at a press conference: "When you see…an entire nation, simultaneously grappling with an extraordinary crisis seated in 400 years of American racism, I'm sorry, that is not the same question as the understandably aggrieved store owner or the devout religious person who wants to go back to services."[61]

Ironically, protests are the exact kind of behavior de Blasio thought should be avoided when he initially downplayed the virus. On March 9, de Blasio said that the virus could only be spread by people in close proximity, such as "two people deep in conversation." He added, "It's not people in the stadium, it's not people in the big open area or a conference at all. It's people close up to each other, deeply engaging each other to the point that the inadvertent spitting that comes with a conversation sometimes, or a sneeze or a cough, directly goes at the other person in close proximity." Certainly, the kind of cult-like chanting that occurred at these rallies meets that criteria.[62]

Does de Blasio think that the coronavirus is the world's first socially conscious virus? Apparently not, because de Blasio then proceeded to instruct NYC's coronavirus contract tracers to not ask those testing positive if they attended a recent BLM

---

61 Zachary Evans, "'Not the Same Question': De Blasio Says Businesses, Churches to Remain Closed Even as Demonstrators Flout Lockdowns," *National Review,* June 2, 2020, https://www.nationalreview.com/news/not-the-same-question-de-blasio-says-businesses-churches-to-remain-closed-even-as-demonstrators-flout-lockdowns/.

62 Aaron Blake and JM Rieger, "New York Mayor Bill de Blasio's Repeated Comments Downplaying the Coronavirus," *Washington Post,* April 1, 2020, https://www.washingtonpost.com/politics/2020/04/01/new-york-mayor-bill-de-blasios-repeated-comments-downplaying-coronavirus/.

demonstration.[63] Two weeks after those instructions, the media began reporting that there wasn't an increase in cases in NYC linked to the protests. If Black Lives Matter is the new national religion, millions congregating without spreading the coronavirus must be its first miracle.

De Blasio spokesperson Avery Cohen told *The City* that "no person will be asked proactively if they attended a protest."[64] This came after Cuomo himself said that "[there's] one variable in this equation that we're not sure of: We don't know what the effect of those protests are"—and de Blasio would rather not know.

Meanwhile, the media attempted to pretend that the medical community suddenly backtracked on social distancing—for this one specific type of activity. An open letter reportedly signed by over one thousand "public health professionals, infectious diseases professionals, and community stakeholders" arguing that it's OK to protest because racism itself is a public health issue was lauded in the media.

That didn't make much sense because the social justice crowd had previously made coronavirus a "racial justice" issue due to its disproportionately killing African Americans (who have more underlying health conditions). By early August, one

---

63   Tobias Hoonhout, "De Blasio Tells Covid Contract Tracers Not to Ask Positive Cases if They've Attended BLM Protests," *National Review,* June 15, 2020, https://www.nationalreview.com/news/de-blasio-tells-covid-contract-tracers-not-to-ask-positive-cases-if-theyve-attended-blm-protests/.

64   Greg B. Smith, "NYC COVID-19 Contact Tracers Not Asking about George Floyd Protest Participation, Despite Fears of New Virus Wave," The City, June 14, 2020, https://www.thecity.nyc/coronavirus/2020/6/14/21290963/nyc-covid-19-trackers-skipping-floyd-protest-questions-even-amid-fears-of-new-wave.

in 1,250 African Americans in the entire country had died from the virus.[65] Even if police killings of unarmed black men were reduced from ten in 2019 to zero, it would take over a century for that to equal six months' worth of coronavirus deaths in the black community.

Regarding another inconsistency in their logic, *National Review*'s Jason Richwine writes:

> Let's take that argument seriously for a moment and ask a follow-up question: Why, then, was there so much criticism of the anti-lockdown protests? The premise of those protests was that continuing lockdowns caused far more economic damage than was necessary. If anything is a public-health issue, surely record unemployment, social isolation, and bans on people going to hospitals for non-urgent care should count.[66]

The response from the supposed medical professionals is "…[W]e do not condemn these [anti-racism] gatherings as risky for COVID-19 transmission. We support them as vital to the national public health and to the threatened health specifically of Black people in the United States…This should not be confused with a permissive stance on all gatherings, particularly protests against stay-home orders. Those actions not only oppose public health interventions but are also rooted in white nationalism and run contrary to respect for Black lives."

---

65 "The Color of Coronavirus: COVID-19 Deaths by Race and Ethnicity in the U.S.," APM Research Lab, August 19, 2020, https://www.apmresearch lab.org/covid/deaths-by-race.

66 Jason Richwine, "1,288 'Public Health Professionals' Disgrace Their Profession," *National Review*, June 4, 2020, https://www.nationalreview.com/corner/1288-public-health-professionals-disgrace-their-profession/.

And they even acknowledge that an increase in infections is to be expected (and as I just noted, the costs would outweigh even a 100 percent reduction in police killings): "Prepare for an increased number of infections in the days following a protest," the letter says. "Provide increased access to testing and care for people in the affected communities, especially when they or their family members put themselves at risk by attending protests."

They did recommend that protesters distance at least six feet between each other "where possible," which is nowhere. Anyone who saw an aerial shot of the protests in any major city knows there was no social distancing.

Andrew Cuomo at least deserves some credit for *eventually* discouraging protests, but he still allowed them to happen in the first place, and we all know he would not give a grace period of a few days before complaining if businesses began reopening en masse.

"We're talking about reopening in one week in New York City and now we're seeing these mass gatherings over the past several nights that could in fact exacerbate the Covid-19 spread," he said in a news conference on June 1st.

"We spent all this time closed down, locked down, masked, socially distanced and then you turn on the TV and you see these mass gatherings that could potentially be infecting hundreds and hundreds of people after everything that we have done.

"This is not helping end coronavirus," Cuomo continued. "I think this has been counterproductive for New York City in many ways."[67]

---

67   Will Feuer and Noah Higgins-Dunn, "New York Gov. Cuomo Says George Floyd Protests Were 'Counterproductive,' Could Exacerbate Coronavirus Outbreak," CNBC, June 1, 2020, https://www.cnbc.com/2020/06/01/new-york-gov-cuomo-says-weekend-protests-were-counterproductive-could-exacerbate-coronavirus-outbreak.html.

While de Blasio and many other liberal mayors ignored the role that protests played in spreading coronavirus, not all chose to ignore reality.

Two days after claiming there wasn't "any conclusive evidence" showing a connection between protests and an increase in cases, Los Angeles Mayor Eric Garcetti acknowledged the protests were "likely" causing the spike in cases—but justified it because the protests were part of a "historic moment."[68]

Miami-Dade County Mayor Carlos A. Giménez cited the protests as a "contributing factor" to the spike in his county. His spokesperson, Patty Abril, said, "Those experts have told him that, based on information in our local emergency rooms, the protests were a contributing factor, along with our community letting its guard down and not social distancing or wearing masks, as mandated. Graduation parties, house parties and restaurants illegally turning into clubs after midnight all contributed to the spike."

When Fox News' Gregg Re reached out to Seattle Mayor Jenny Durkan's office for comment, he was directed to health official James Apa, who acknowledged that the protests "may have" played a role in new cases—but otherwise attempted to downplay it.

A study published in Oxford University's *Journal of Public Health* confirmed as much, that cities with protests involving over ten thousand attendees saw massive spikes in the spread of coronavirus. While New York City wasn't included in the study, it did find that the virus's spread was 20 percent higher than it

---

68 Gregg Re, "Anti-Police Demonstrations May Have Sparked New Coronavirus Cases, Some Cities Now Acknowledge," Fox News, July 6, 2020, https://www.foxnews.com/politics/cities-protests-coronavirus-cases-black-lives-matter.

was expected to be in Houston, 34 percent higher in Jacksonville, and 53 percent higher in Orlando, to give just a few examples.[69] The only exceptions were cities that were previously hotspots, indicating that herd immunity helped stop the spread. And to be fair, NYC could fall into that category, but the point here is the hypocrisy both in NYC and among liberals nationally.

De Blasio made his double standard explicit in July, cancelling all large events through September, but making an exception for Black Lives Matter, and Black Lives Matter only. "This is a historic moment of change. We have to respect that but also say to people the kinds of gatherings we're used to, the parades, the fairs—we just can't have that while we're focusing on health right now," he told CNN's Wolf Blitzer.

His carefree approach applies solely to that group.

In mid-April, de Blasio increased the fine individuals would face if they failed to social distance properly to $1,000, which was later enforced against a grand total of zero protesters.[70]

When it came to Jewish communities holding funerals and attending religious services, he explicitly called them out. After breaking up a Jewish funeral, in a tweet dated April 28 he wrote: "My message to the Jewish community, and all communities, is this simple: the time for warnings has passed. I have instructed the NYPD to proceed immediately to summons or even arrest

---

Randall Valentine et al., "Relationship of George Floyd Protests to Increases in COVID-19 Cases Using Event Study Methodology," *Oxford Academic Journal of Public Health,* August 5, 2020, https://academic.oup.com/jpubhealth/advance-article/doi/10.1093/pubmed/fdaa127/5880636.

70 Shant Shahrigian, "New York City Increases Social Distancing Fines to $1,000, Mayor de Blasio Says," *Daily News,* April 19, 2020, https://www.nydailynews.com/coronavirus/ny-coronavirus-new-york-city-social-distancing-fines-20200419-qh6byaupc5bo5fcr4w4pky52by-story.html.

those who gather in large groups. This is about stopping this disease and saving lives. Period."[71] The tweet, which many accused of being anti-Semitic, was made days after the city announced they'd provide five hundred thousand free meals to Muslims for Ramadan.[72]

In his defense, de Blasio claimed that he was not singling out the Jewish community for criticism, because no large gatherings are allowed—at least for another month, provided they gather for a cause he agrees with. "We are talking about thousands of people in close proximity in one site. We will never ever allow something like that to go unchecked anywhere," he unprophetically declared.[73]

When it came to religious services more generally, de Blasio said that comparing them to protests is like "comparing apples and oranges." He later told CNN that "the protests were an entirely different reality, a national phenomenon, that was not something that the government could just say, go away." He may have a case

---

71 @NYCMayor, "My message to the Jewish community, and all communities, is this simple: the time for warnings has passed. I have instructed the NYPD to proceed immediately to summons or even arrest those who gather in large groups. This is about stopping this disease and saving lives. Period," Twitter, April 28, 2020, 8:35 p.m., https://twitter.com/nycmayor/status/1255309615883063297?lang=en.

72 Henry Goldman, "NYC to Serve 500,000 Free Halal Meals to Muslims During Ramadan," Bloomberg, April 23, 2020, https://www.bloomberg.com/news/articles/2020-04-23/nyc-to-serve-500-000-free-halal-meals-to-muslims-during-ramadan.

73 Noah Higgins-Dunn and Marty Steinberg, "Orthodox Jewish Funeral That Drew Thousands Was 'Absolutely Unacceptable,' NYC Mayor Says," CNBC, April 29, 2020, https://www.cnbc.com/2020/04/29/orthodox-jewish-funeral-that-drew-thousands-was-absolutely-unacceptable-nyc-mayor-says.html.

there if: 1) he didn't preside over the largest police force in the world, and 2) he didn't personally encourage the protests.[74]

When it came to people going to the beach in May (where it isn't difficult to socially distance), de Blasio threatened to personally have beachgoers "taken right out of the water."[75]

On May 28, two days after the George Floyd protests began nationwide, de Blasio warned so-called nonessential businesses from reopening early, telling them without a hint of irony, "We're in the middle of a pandemic, we're in the middle of a crisis. The only way we have gotten things together is by sticking together and following the rules."[76] The businesses NY specifically labeled as nonessential included theaters, event venues, anything that facilitated gambling, indoor portions of shopping malls, gyms, places of public amusement, and barber shops, among other similarly themed businesses.[77]

The spread may have been less in New York, but only because of how hard they had already been hit by the virus, producing

---

74   Ian Hanchett, "De Blasio: Comparing Protests to Religious Services 'Apples to Oranges,'" Breitbart, July 2, 2020, https://www.breitbart.com/clips/2020/07/02/de-blasio-comparing-protests-to-religious-services-apples-and-oranges/.

75   Zack Budryk, "De Blasio: Swimmers at New York City Beaches Will Be 'Taken Right Out of the Water,'" The Hill, May 18, 2020, https://thehill.com/homenews/state-watch/498331-de-blasio-swimmers-at-new-york-city-beaches-will-be-taken-right-out-of.

76   Kristine Garcia, "Nonessential Businesses Can't 'Jump the Gun' on Reopening; Fines Will Be Issued, de Blasio Says," WPIX, May 28, 2020, https://www.pix11.com/news/coronavirus/nonessential-businesses-that-reopen-without-permission-will-be-fined-de-blasio-says.

77   Allan S. Bloom and Arielle E. Kobetz, "New York State Issues Updated Guidance on Essential (and Non-Essential) Businesses," National Law Review, April 9, 2020, https://www.natlawreview.com/article/new-york-state-issues-updated-guidance-essential-and-non-essential-businesses.

some level of herd immunity. But the increase in cases nation-wide coincides with the protests, and the hypocrisy is impossible to ignore.

AS NEW YORK BURNS, THE MEDIA SINGS CUOMO'S PRAISES

Truth be damned, Cuomo is fortunate to live in a world where the entirety of the mainstream media (minus one network) sides with him ideologically. Only at CNN and MSNBC would you see pundits blast Trump for the rising coronavirus caseloads and death count while simultaneously praising Cuomo's response—even as the majority of those cases and deaths were in New York.

After the virus had killed thirty-two thousand New York residents (24 percent of the nation's total deaths at the time, within less than 6 percent of the nation's population), Cuomo declared on July 13 that "Trump's COVID scandal makes what Nixon did at Watergate look innocent."[78]

Chuck Todd let Cuomo spin the facts on nursing homes unchallenged in a June 28 appearance, long after the facts were already well established. "And final question, we talked about this, about nursing homes before, and you've taken some heat on the directive and you said you were following a national directive. But let me ask it again, similarly at this point, do you think these senior centers are safe, period?" Todd asked.

Cuomo replied by arguing that New York was beating the national average when it came to nursing homes. "Almost 50

---

78   Dan Clark, "Cuomo: Trump's COVID-19 Response Makes Nixon Look 'Innocent,'" WRVO Public Radio, July 13, 2020, https://www.wrvo.org/post/cuomo-trumps-covid-19-response-makes-nixon-look-innocent.

percent of the deaths…but in New York, we're number 46 in the nation in terms of percentage of deaths at nursing homes compared to the total percentage. By *The New York Times*, we're number 46." The *New York Times* report he was quoting included the disclaimer that New York hasn't been fully reporting its data: "In New York, the case count is often the same as the death count because the state only reports the number of people who have died but not the number of overall infections."[79] And as we also know, the nursing home death numbers Cuomo is basing this claim on are likely half the true death toll because hospital deaths of nursing home patients weren't counted.

Furthermore, as NewsBusters' Nicholas Fondacaro notes:

> In crunching the numbers presented by *The Times*, NewsBusters has figured out that New York's nursing home death rate compared to infections was 90 percent. New York reports 7,177 nursing home infections compared to 6,432 nursing home deaths. No other state came close to matching that rate.

> Democratic-controlled states like California (23,646), Illinois (21,390), and New Jersey (36,316) all had massive numbers of nursing home infections. But their number of deaths (CA-2,832; IL-3,649; NJ-6,617) didn't match infections as closely as New York's did.

> Comparing nursing home deaths as a percentage of total deaths, as Cuomo was leaning on, was a bit of an apples-to-oranges comparison. Those living in nursing homes

---

79   Nicholas Fondacaro, "Todd Lets Cuomo Twist Truth on NY Nursing Home Deaths, Lecture FL/TX," MRC NewsBusters, June 18, 2020, https://www.newsbusters.org/blogs/nb/nicholas-fondacaro/2020/06/28/ todd-lets-cuomo-twist-truth-ny-nursing-home-deaths-lecture.

usually needed more assistance and had more health conditions that made them vulnerable to the virus. Meanwhile, the general population contained other people (elderly and otherwise) who were also vulnerable. And obviously, more people live outside nursing homes than in them.

That's not to mention that Cuomo had disastrously ordered infected elderly patients to be returned to their assisted living facilities, thus spreading the virus.

Ironically, the whole conversation was regarding Florida seeing a spike in cases, though the duo didn't see it notable to mention that Florida's daily coronavirus deaths were still consistently falling because the average age of those infected had fallen into the thirties.[80] A full two months after the interview aired, New York still had three times as many coronavirus deaths per capita as Florida.

Although that interview did occur at a time when NY's deaths and cases were falling while Florida's cases (and only cases) were rising, that's simply because New York was hit first by the virus and then proceeded to export it to states like Florida. This logic would be like saying a student who went from getting straight Ds to straight Bs is a better student than someone who went from getting straight Bs to straight As because he was more improved.

When Cuomo appeared on ABC's *Good Morning America* in mid-June, the host Amy Robach gushed over him without a single mention of the nursing home scandal. "You've been commended

---

80   Daniel Horowitz, "Horowitz: All the Ways the Media Is Misleading You about a Record Spike in Florida," TheBlaze, June 22, 2020, https://www.theblaze.com/op-ed/horowitz-all-the-ways-the-media-is-misleading-you-about-a-record-spike-in-florida.

for your clear and your calm leadership. People from all over the country and the world have tuned in to your press conferences. Your statewide approval rating, a career high, 84%. You came in second only to President Obama as the most trusted democratic leader in America. How do you intend on spending that political capital that you've earned?" asked the host.[81]

Over at CNN in late June, guest Juliette Kayyem criticized Florida's handling of the virus, apparently unaware that New York had ten times as many deaths as Florida on a per capita basis at the time of her appearance. Then she praised Cuomo. "For a long time, Governor Cuomo in New York I think has aggressively, even if belated, tried to fight the virus statewide. In other words, statewide rules that were trying to drill down, bring down the number, save the hospitals, and also have surge capacity. What you've seen from DeSantis, the governor of Florida, is essentially a lot like Trump, just sort of ignore the problem, we can handle it, not a big deal, no statewide rules, no statewide orders, and then, then you start to see the numbers."[82]

Cuomo also had the assistance of "brother Fredo," who at least acknowledged the nursing home scandal existed before dismissing it entirely. "Nursing homes, people died there. They didn't have to, it was mismanaged and the operators have been given immunity. What do you have to say about that?" asked his

81 Kristine Marsh, "Adoring ABC Swoons Over 'Luv Guv' Cuomo; NO Mention of Nursing Home Scandal," MRC NewsBusters, June 17, 2020, https://www.newsbusters.org/blogs/nb/kristine-marsh/2020/06/17/adoring-abc-swoons-over-luv-guv-cuomo-no-mention-nursing-home.

82 Duncan Schroeder, "CNN's Kayyem Praises Andrew Cuomo's Disastrous 'Leadership,' Bashes DeSantis," MRC NewsBusters, June 25, 2020, https://www.newsbusters.org/blogs/nb/duncan-schroeder/2020/06/25/cnns-kayyem-praises-andrew-cuomos-disastrous-leadership-bashes.

brother Chris. Andrew responded by deflecting blame, saying that nursing home operators have very strict rules to follow and that they'll be held accountable if they broke the law. Many of those "strict rules" were the ones that created the crisis itself.

While that answer in no way explains why Andrew forced nursing homes to accept coronavirus patients, Chris responded with brotherly love: "I'm wowed by what you did, and more importantly, I'm wowed by how you did it. This was very hard. I know it's not over. But obviously, I love you as a brother, obviously, I'll never be objective, obviously, I think you're the best politician in the country. But I hope you feel good about what you did for your people because I know they appreciate it."[83]

CBS managed to gush over Andrew more than his brother, proclaiming that he was "having a moment"—and informed the audience that he's single.[84]

NBC's Savannah Guthrie asked Cuomo about nursing homes. "In retrospect, was that order a mistake? I know that guidance has since been changed," to which Cuomo responded by lying again that his state had a lower percentage of people dying in nursing homes than other states.[85] He then blamed Europe for

---

83 Nicholas Fondacaro, "CNN's Cuomo Dismisses Blood on Brother's Hands, Admits He's Not 'Objective,'" MRC NewsBusters, June 24, 2020, https://www.newsbusters.org/blogs/nb/nicholas-fondacaro/2020/06/24/cnns-cuomo-dismisses-blood-brothers-hands-admits-hes-not.

84 Nicholas Fondacaro, "CBS's Pauley Gushes for Cuomo: He's 'Having a Moment' and Single!" MRC NewsBusters, June 21, 2020, https://www.newsbusters.org/blogs/nb/nicholas-fondacaro/2020/06/21/cbss-pauley-gushes-cuomo-hes-having-moment-and-single.

85 Kyle Drennen, "NBC to Cuomo: 'Mistake' to Force COVID Patients into Nursing Homes?" MRC NewsBusters, June 23, 2020, https://www.newsbusters.org/blogs/nb/kyle-drennen/2020/06/23/nbc-cuomo-mistake-force-covid-patients-nursing-homes.

the virus, and Guthrie moved on to a different question about taking down statues instead of offering pushback.[86]

By July Cuomo upped the ante, going as far as to claim that President Trump didn't think the coronavirus existed. "Do one simple thing: acknowledge to the American people that Covid exists. It is a major problem. It's going to continue until we admit it and each of us stands up to do our part," Cuomo said. "If he does not acknowledge that, then he is facilitating the virus. He is enabling the virus."[87] If only de Blasio had acknowledged the virus existed.

While Cuomo accused Trump of failing to acknowledge the existence of the virus, the media brazenly failed to acknowledge the existence of Cuomo's own failures.

Despite the nonsensical media coverage, it worked. Thanks to a fawning liberal media, being wrong as a liberal in power is just like being a weatherman; there are no consequences for being wrong.

Just over a month after the nursing home order was implemented, Cuomo's approval hit a new record high at 77 percent. Respondents had three times as much trust in Cuomo than President Trump.[88]

And in a *New York Times* article about the response of the two stooges, we learn how shameless they are: "The governor and the

---

86 Drennen.

87 Ken Meyer, "Gov. Cuomo Slams 'Co-Conspirator of Covid' Trump for Downplaying Pandemic: 'He Is Enabling the Virus,'" Mediaite, July 6, 2020, https://www.mediaite.com/tv/gov-cuomo-slams-co-conspirator-of-covid-trump-for-downplaying-pandemic-he-is-enabling-the-virus/.

88 Karen Dewitt, WAMC Public Radio, April 27, 2020, https://www.wamc.org/post/cuomo-approval-rating-77-amid-covid-19-pandemic.

mayor emphasized that they had no misgivings about their initial handling of the response."[89]

When they suffer no consequences for being wrong, why would they?

---

89   J. David Goodman, "How Delays and Unheeded Warnings Hindered New York's Virus Fight," New York Times, April 8, 2020, updated July 18, 2020, https://www.nytimes.com/2020/04/08/nyregion/new-york-coronavirus-response-delays.html.

THE ECONOMICS OF NEW YORK

Throughout the nineteenth century, the vast majority of those immigrating to America entered through New York.

While millions around the world found New York as a refuge—a land of opportunity—today the state is producing refugees of its own in the form of millions of citizens fleeing for other states. Americans have been migrating on net from Blue States to Red States at a pace of one thousand people per day, and New York leads the pack.[90]

The state has become antithetical to the promise of liberty and upward mobility, plagued by a massive, inefficient government,

---

90   Joel Griffith, "1,000 People a Day: Why Red States Are Getting Richer and Blue States Poorer," The Heritage Foundation, May 5, 2015, https://www.heritage.org/government-regulation/report/1000-people-day-why-red-states-are-getting-richer-and-blue-states.

high taxes, excessive regulations, a high cost of living, degrading infrastructure, and incompetent leadership.

New York Governor Andrew Cuomo can at least use the excuse that he's merely continuing the bad policies that have doomed the state. In the Big Apple, Mayor Bill de Blasio actively works to implement a progressive agenda to "dismantle" policies that have produced prosperity, and the consequences are becoming evident. While New York State has been hemorrhaging residents over the past decade, the city housing nearly half of its residents managed to buck that trend—until de Blasio became mayor.

Whether the city will bounce back has been the subject of much debate recently. With de Blasio as mayor, the answer is unquestionably "no." As the entrepreneur James Altucher points out, even throughout the crime wave of the 1970s and '80s, New York "was still the capital of the business world (meaning, it was the primary place young people would go to build wealth and find opportunity). It was culturally on top of its game—home to artists, theater, media, advertising, publishing. And it was probably the food capital of the U.S."[91]

With strict lockdown rules crippling business still in effect even as the city goes days without a single coronavirus death, many wealthy who can work remotely have fled, restaurants have been crippled, and Broadway has gone dark.

THE STATE OF THE STATE

If you're looking to live in a free state, New York should be the last on your list—literally.

---

91   James Altucher, "NYC Is Dead Forever… Here's Why," JamesAltucher. com, August 13, 2020, https://jamesaltucher.com/blog/nyc-is-dead-forever-heres-why/.

A handful of studies have examined the freedom of the fifty states—and no matter which you look at, New York ranks dead last.

On the Cato Institute's "Freedom in the 50 States" study, New York ranked last, both overall and on most of the individual criteria used to come to that ranking. New York ranked last in fiscal policy (which relates to how high taxes are, how many government employees there are, how much it spends, and how much debt it has), regulatory freedom, economic freedom, and lawsuit freedom. The state didn't fare much better on its other metrics: fortieth in personal freedom, forty-sixth in land use freedom, thirty-seventh in education, and forty-first in occupational freedom.[92]

The Mercatus Center's "Freedom in the 50 States" study yielded similar results, with New York ranking as the worst state in which to reside. It ranked fiftieth in fiscal policy and economic freedom, forty-fourth in regulatory policy, and forty-eighth in personal freedom. As the study notes:

> New York is by far the least free state in the Union. One of us lives in New York and can attest to the fact that few New Yorkers would be surprised by such a finding. Sadly, equally few New Yorkers seem to believe that anything can be done about the situation. New York has the highest taxes in the country. Property, selective sales, individual income, and corporate income taxes are particularly high. Spending on social services and "other" is well above national norms. Only Massachusetts has

---

92 "Freedom in the 50 States Index," Cato Institute, 2020, https://www.freedominthe50states.org/how-its-calculated.

more government debt as a percentage of the economy. Government employment is higher than average. On personal freedoms, gun laws are extremely restrictive. Motorists are highly regulated, but several kinds of gambling are allowed statewide (not casinos, except on reservations). Home school regulations are burdensome. Along with Vermont, New York has the strictest health insurance community rating regulations. Mandated coverages are also very high. Eminent domain is totally unreformed. Perversely, the state strictly limits what grassroots PACs may give to candidates and parties, but not what corporations and unions may give.[93]

While the focus of this book is on New York City and the state it's named after, the policies that have doomed them aren't specific to that state. Mercatus found that the percentage of voters going Blue in presidential elections (which is an indicator of how they vote in state and local elections) correlates inversely with how free a state is. An unfortunate reality is that many of those fleeing Blue States are taking the same politics with them that doomed the places they fled.

A study from Truth in Accounting analyzed the fiscal health of the fifty states, and the trend was clear—that the more Republican control, the better (or less-worse) fiscal health those states are in.[94]

---

93 William P. Ruger and Jason Sorens, "Freedom in the 50 States: An Index of Personal and Economic Freedom," Mercatus Center: George Mason University, February 2009, https://www.mercatus.org/system/files/ Freedom_in_the_50_States.pdf.

94 *Financial State of the States: An Annual Report by Truth in Accounting*, Truth in Accounting, September 2019, https://www.truthinaccounting. org/library/doclib/FSOS-booklet-2019.pdf.

The worst run states and their unfunded liabilities per citizen, according to its "2019 Financial State of the States," are:

- New Jersey, -$65,100
- Illinois, -$52,600
- Connecticut, -$51,800
- Massachusetts, -$31,200
- Hawaii, -$31,200
- Delaware, -$27,100
- Kentucky, -$25,700
- California, -$21,800
- New York, -$20,500
- Vermont, -$19,000

At least New York wasn't ranked dead last that time, but they weren't far from it.

The best states actually had a surplus per citizen. They are:

- Alaska, $74,200 per taxpayer
- North Dakota, $30,700
- Wyoming, $20,800
- Utah, $5,300
- Idaho, $2,900
- Tennessee, $2,800
- South Dakota, $2,800
- Nebraska, $2,000
- Oregon, $1,600
- Iowa, $700

Alaska is an outlier due to oil wealth combined with a low population, and has a split legislature with a Republican governor.

Every single other state with the exception of Oregon has a Republican governor and legislature. Nebraska is technically an exception in that it is the only state with a unicameral legislature, but it is Republican controlled.

New York's Regulatory Climate

Due to the cost of compliance, from the perspective of a business, regulations are simply taxes by another name. While few disagree that there's a need for basic regulatory standards to safeguard consumers, New York and New York City have created a regulatory labyrinth for businesses to navigate.

New York ranks forty-first (with fiftieth being the worst) in the Pacific Research Institute's 50-State Small Business Index. These rankings take into account a litany of regulations and their costs, including workers compensation insurance, unemployment insurance, short-term disability insurance requirements, minimum wage laws, right-to-work laws, occupational licensing laws, land use regulations, energy regulations, tort liability costs, telecommunications regulations, start-up and filing costs, and more.[95]

In addition to all the state regulations, de Blasio has further added to them in his city. Among the new business regulations implemented by his administration are:

Lactation Rooms: yes, really. As if NYC retail space isn't expensive enough, businesses with four or more employees are required to provide "lactation room accommodations." In addition to having a specific lactation room, businesses must also

---

95   Wayne Winegarden, "The 50-State Small Business Regulation Index," Pacific Research Institute, July 2015, https://www.pacificresearch.org/wp-content/uploads/2017/04/SmBusinessIndex_UpdatedVersion2_web.pdf.

"provide adequate time for employees to express breast milk during the workday," and have a "written policy on lactation accommodations."[96] All the specifics of this regulation span a total of over four thousand words. It must be particularly fun for small all-male companies to comply with this.

- Predictive Scheduling: Those in the food and retail sector with more than twenty employees now must give each employee their final schedule at least seventy-two hours before it's to take effect. After it's issued, employers cannot make any changes, such as adding or removing shifts. Employers are required to keep at least three years of records of employee work schedules to comply with this regulation. The law prohibits employers from scheduling an employee to work two shifts over two days with less than eleven hours between shifts unless they get written consent from workers and pay them an extra one hundred dollars for the second shift. Further complicating things, it also outlaws having "on call" shifts, which would be needed to fill an unexpected vacancy. New York State at least saw these kinds of regulations as absurd and ended up cancelling its plans to implement them after receiving feedback that highlighted "significant issues" with the policy.[97]

- Congestion Pricing: This doesn't take effect until 2021 but is guaranteed to damage the city's businesses simply

---

96   "Frequently Asked Questions," New York City Human Rights, https://www1.nyc.gov/site/cchr/law/lactation-faqs.page.

97   Dena Calo and Gillian Cooper, "New York State Cancels Predictive Scheduling Regulations," JD Supra, March 15, 2019, https://www.jdsupra.com/legalnews/new-york-state-cancels-predictive-56429/.

by reducing the number of people participating in the economy. While the size of the toll isn't known yet, it's expected to be around $14 (in addition to all other tolls) and will be paid by businesses entering Manhattan below 60th Street.

- Paid Time Off: Rather than have employers who can afford it offer it as a perk, de Blasio wants to increase the amount of time workers get paid to do nothing. De Blasio made a push for every worker at firms with five or more employees to receive ten days' paid time off, which would affect roughly five hundred thousand employees. While de Blasio promised this would be implemented by the end of 2019, several delays prevented that. By the end of the year, de Blasio said he thinks he will pass a bill to implement it relatively soon, but the pandemic has derailed that, at least for now.[98]

And he passed a fifteen-dollar minimum wage, which I'm sure in only a few short years will itself be deemed "poverty wages" by minimum wage advocates.

That the minimum wage costs jobs is a position held by the overwhelming majority of economists, but as usual, facts seldom get in the way of the left's narrative.

The minimum wage for fast food workers specifically in New York City was ratcheted up under de Blasio, increasing from $10.50 in 2015 to $12 by the end of 2016, to $13.50 by the end of 2017, and up to $15 by the end of 2018. New York State will have a

---

98 Erin Durkin, "Paid Vacation Legislation Stalls Short of Finish Line, Despite Mayoral Push," Politico, December 9, 2019, https://www.politico.com/states/new-york/albany/story/2019/12/06/paid-vacation-legislation-stalls-short-of-finish-line-despite-mayoral-push-1231058.

$15 minimum wage in 2021. Those increases corresponded with a drop in employment in the city's restaurant industry that (until the coronavirus pandemic) paralleled only the drop in that sector's employment during the great recession of 2008–09.

As the Foundation for Economic Education's Mark Perry writes:

> The current state minimum wage outside of NYC is $11.10 an hour [in 2019], so employers in the city are faced with paying a large 35 percent wage premium compared to their counterparts outside of the metro area for low-skilled workers. And it's having a devastating effect on the city's small businesses and restaurants.[99]
>
> Compared to the first half of last year when there was an average of about 318,000 restaurant jobs in the city, there were only slightly more than 314,000 restaurant employees during the same period this year, representing a loss of nearly 4,000 food jobs over the last year at a rate of 11 jobs lost on average every day.

Perry also notes that the president of the Queens Chamber of Commerce said he has seen an uptick in small-business closures, and he attributed it to the minimum-wage legislation. "They're cutting their staff. They're cutting their hours. They're shutting down," he said. "It's not just the rent."

Crain's New York Business reported in April 2019 that:

---

99   Mark J. Perry, "NYC Has Lost 4,000 Jobs in the Restaurant Sector Alone in the Last Year," Foundation for Economic Education, August 12, 2019, https://fee.org/articles/nyc-has-lost-4-000-jobs-in-the-restaurant-sector-alone-in-the-last-year/.

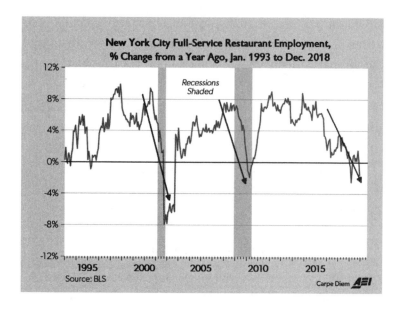

New York City Full-Service Restaurant Employment, % Change from a Year Ago, Jan. 1993 to Dec. 2018

Last year the city lost about 6,000 restaurant jobs, a decline of 3.4%, according to an analysis by the Independent Budget Office, which used seasonally adjusted numbers for the fourth quarter, marking the first time in more than a decade that jobs in the industry declined.[100]

While such an analysis doesn't exist of NYC, evidence from Seattle indicates that a fifteen dollar minimum wage ends up costing workers, on net.

A study conducted by the University of Washington found that the law reduced hours by 9 percent and led to benefit cuts, which caused incomes to fall on net by 6 percent. And the kicker? That study was conducted when

---

100 Lizeth Beltran, "Restaurant Jobs on the Decline," *Crain's: A New York Business,* April 2, 2019, https://www.crainsnewyork.com/food-beverage/restaurant-jobs-decline.

Seattle's minimum wage had "only" risen from $10.50 to $13 an hour, as the $15 wage was phased in gradually. Despite that $2.50 an hour raise at the time of the study, workers were still $125 a month worse off.

And that's for the people who kept their jobs. Things were much worse for the five thousand workers who lost their jobs entirely.[101]

De Blasio said at a Fight for Fifteen rally that "we're not going to have a city where people are below the poverty line when we can lift them up with a decent minimum wage,"[102] but all evidence suggests that for most, poverty isn't a wage problem, it's a work problem.

In 2015, only 11 percent of (working age) people in poverty worked full time. By contrast, 63 percent of those in poverty don't work at all.[103] Of full-time workers in America, only 2 percent live in poverty (compared to 32 percent of the unemployed).[104]

Income and Wealth

The high cost of living in New York helps mask the true extent of poverty in the state. If a state has a cost of living double the

---

101 Carl Campanile, "Study Reveals Workers Earn Less After Minimum Wage Hike," *New York Post*, June 26, 2017, https://nypost.com/2017/06/26/study-reveals-workers-earn-less-after-minimum-wage-hike/.

102 "Transcript: Mayor de Blasio Delivers Remarks at Fight for $15 Rally," Official Website of the City of New York, November 10, 2015, https://www1.nyc.gov/office-of-the-mayor/news/805-15/transcript-mayor-de-blasio-delivers-remarks-fight-15-rally.

103 Preston Cooper, "Sorry, Bernie, Few Full-Time Workers Live in Poverty," Economics 21, October 13, 2016, https://economics21.org/html/sorry-bernie-few-full-time-workers-live-poverty-2094.html.

104 Ben Gitis, "Primer: Minimum Wage and Combating Poverty," American Action Forum, December 3, 2013, https://www.americanactionforum.org/research/primer-minimum-wage-and-combating-poverty/.

national average and its residents earn 80 percent more than the national average, its residents may appear 80 percent wealthier than the average citizen nationwide but are actually poorer.

Nominally speaking, New York ranks thirty-two overall in poverty, but after adjusting for the cost of living, it rises to seventh place with 18.1 percent of citizens in poverty. One hundred dollars in the average state only spends like $86.43 in New York.[105] In addition to high taxes, that's a 14 percent "cost of living" tax for the privilege of living in the state on top of it all. In New York City, where rent costs more than double the national median, it's even more expensive.[106]

Kristin Tate notes in her book *The Liberal Invasion of Red State America* that:

> In New York since 2010, job growth in Upstate New York
> is less than a third of the average in New York City and
> just a third of the national average. In fact, in 21 Upstate
> counties, the local economies have not recovered to their
> job rates from before the Great Recession. If Upstate
> New York was ranked among all states, it would cur-
> rently rank 47th in the union since 2010 in job creation.
> Five counties have experienced negative GDP growth
> since the recession while even the fastest growing region

---

105 Kristin Tate, *The Liberal Invasion of Red State America* (Washington, DC: Regnery Publishing, 2020), 24–25.

106 Hillary Hoffower and Libertina Brandt, "13 Mind-Blowing Facts That Show Just How Expensive New York City Really Is," Business Insider, November 15, 2019, https://www.businessinsider.com/how-expensive-is-new-york-city-mind-blowing-facts-2019-6#3-the-median-rent-for-a-two-bedroom-apartment-in-new-york-city-is-3500-over-two-times-the-national-median-of-1480-4.

north of NYC is expanding at only half of the rate of the national average.[107]

Only for a single year (2012) since Cuomo took office in 2011 did New York's GDP growth exceed the national average.[108] New York City's economy lagged behind the national average under de Blasio until he effectively got a bailout from Trump, with the banking sector (which benefitted handsomely from Trump's corporate tax cuts and deregulatory policies) driving growth.[109] De Blasio's response to the pandemic has reversed his luck on that front.

The Infrastructure of New York

All the supposed benefits of high taxes claimed by liberals have yet to be realized in New York. The clichéd arguments that high taxes are needed for high quality schools and infrastructure have already been proven otherwise for the former, and the same is true for the latter.

Just as important as the distinction between big government vs. small government is efficient government vs. inefficient government. And New York has the worst of both worlds with a big and massively inefficient government.

---

107   Tate, 105.
108   "Total Gross Domestic Product for New York," FRED, April 7, 2020, https://fred.stlouisfed.org/series/NYNGSP.
109   Will Bredderman, "NYC's Economic Growth Lagged Nation's, New Report Shows," *Crain's: New York Business,* August 13, 2018, https://www.crainsnewyork.com/article/20180813/ECONOMY/180819976/nyc-s-economic-growth-lagged-nation-s-new-report-shows.

A report from the Center for an Urban Future in 2014 painted a crumbling picture of both NYC and NY's infrastructure.[110] The report found

- Eleven percent of NYC's 162 bridges are more than one hundred years old.
- Every day nearly three million cars drive over bridges rated as "fracture critical" and "structurally deficient."
- Of NYC's subway system's 728 miles of mainline signals, 37 percent have exceeded their fifty-year useful life.
- Fifteen percent of the city's 6,800 miles of water mains are over one hundred years old, and in all but one year since 1998 there have been over four hundred water main breaks.
- The average NY gas main is fifty-six years old.
- Of 19,000 lane miles of roads and highways in New York, 30.4 percent are in "fair or "poor" condition. This compares to only 15.7 percent in 2000. NYC's roads are worse, with 28 percent in Brooklyn being rated substandard, 31 percent in Queens, 34 percent in the Bronx, 40 percent in Staten Island, and 43 percent in Manhattan.

In total, the report concluded that bringing the state's infrastructure up to par would take an investment of nearly $50 billion over four to five years.

To fund that, the state merely needs to increase taxes further on top of already having among the highest taxes in the country,

---

110 Raya Jalabi, "New York's Dangerously Old Public Infrastructures," *Guardian*, March 14, 2014, https://www.theguardian.com/world/2014/mar/14/new-yorks-dangerously-old-public-infrastructures.

all while dealing with revenue losses due to the coronavirus. And with New York level inefficiency, it's a guarantee that everything will cost more than expected.

Some historical examples demonstrate this to an absurd extent.

In 1929, the NYC Board of Transportation budgeted $86 million for the then newly-proposed Second Avenue T line, with an estimated completion date of 1938–1941. The Great Depression pushed that estimated opening date back to 1948, and World War II pushed the estimated date of completion back to 1951.[111]

The estimated date of completion continued being pushed back incrementally throughout the century—and even into the next. It wasn't until 2017 that the Second Avenue Subway was opened—and that was just the first phase.

The second phase of the project isn't expected to open until 2027–2029, so perhaps our great-great-great grandchildren will witness that one day.

Another notable example of NYC's incompetence came after the concrete floor of Central Park's Wollman Rink buckled. Initially projected to cost $4.9 million over two years to fix, the city spent the next six years and $13 million ($30 million in 2020 dollars) attempting and failing to do so. Eventually, after he spent much time criticizing the mayor over the debacle, real estate developer Donald Trump (better known for his later work) was given $3 million to fix the rink and a six-month deadline. The rink was fixed in four months, $750,000 under budget.

---

111   Sam Jewler, "The Long, Tortured History of the Second Avenue Subway," *New York Intelligencer,* July 24, 2009, https://nymag.com/intelligencer/2009/07/the_tortured_history_of_the_se.html.

New York's Looming Fiscal Disaster

New York and NYC were already driving on the path to fiscal ruin, and the coronavirus pandemic has kicked it into overdrive.

Not once in nine years as governor has Cuomo attended the annual meeting of the state Financial Control Board (of which he is the chairman). The only other governor since the 1970s who forwent those meetings was Eliot Spitzer.

New York had already faced a projected $4.2 billion budget gap for fiscal year 2022, but that's likely to balloon to somewhere in the ballpark of $6–7 billion due to the pandemic.[112]

For the sake of clarity, a budget gap is not a synonym for a budget deficit. New York isn't like most states, because it lacks a balanced budget amendment requiring a legislature to pass a balanced budget and doesn't have prohibitions on carrying over a deficit. However, while the legislature doesn't have to pass a balanced budget, the budget the governor submits is required to be balanced.[113] In other words, Cuomo will be forced to propose spending cuts and tax hikes, though the legislature may not pass that budget.

And it's looking like the state will weigh tax hikes over spending cuts. Cuomo had technically frozen the wages of state

112 Thomas P. DiNapoli, "DiNapoli: NYC Faces Unprecedented Fiscal and Economic Challenges," August 4, 2020, Office of the New York State Comptroller, https://www.osc.state.ny.us/press/releases/2020/08/dinapoli-nyc-faces-unprecedented-fiscal-and-economic-challenges.

113 "NCSL Fiscal Brief: State Balanced Budget Provisions," National Conference of State Legislatures: the Forum for America's Ideas, October 2010, https://www.ncsl.org/documents/fiscal/StateBalanced BudgetProvisions2010.pdf.

employees on paper for ninety days, but the "freeze" simply defers eventual wage hikes.[114]

According to E.J. McMahon of Empire Center, writing of New York City's finances:

> In [de Blasio's] April budget proposal, the mayor tapped reserve funds, targeted federal coronavirus relief aid and savings from a hiring freeze to close a two-year gap of $8.7 billion. De Blasio also asked the state Legislature for authorization to borrow $7 billion to cover operating expenses—an extreme step for which he could offer no compelling justification. That idea didn't get anywhere in Albany (although Cuomo himself had won authorization to issue up to $11 billion in deficit bonds).
>
> In late May, de Blasio updated his financial plan to reflect a further $1.6 billion drop in revenues, warning the added shortfall might force him to lay off 22,000 city workers.

He made yet another borrowing request to the Legislature—this time seeking to issue $5 billion in deficit bonds over two years, again without demonstrating any immediate need for the money. Again, he was unsuccessful.[115]

While the city is likely to lay off twenty-two thousand municipal workers due to the pandemic cash crunch, they still found

---

114 E.J. McMahon, "Cuomo Extends Slushy 'Freeze' of State Worker Pay," Empire Center, June 30, 2020, https://www.empirecenter.org/publi cations/cuomo-extends-slushy-freeze-of-state-worker-pay/.

115 E.J. McMahon, "Instead of Facing Fiscal Crises, NYC, State Are Burying Their Heads in the Sand," Empire Center, July 2, 2020, https://www. empirecenter.org/publications/instead-of-facing-fiscal-crises-nyc/.

enough money for de Blasio's wife to continue spending $2 million a year on staffers.[116]

Like Cuomo, the ideology of de Blasio suggests that even more tax hikes are to come to his city.

During her presidential campaign, 2016 election silver medalist Hillary Clinton proposed $1 trillion in new taxes (over the next decade). Joe Biden upped the ante in 2020 and pledged at least $4 trillion in new taxes. But to tally up all the taxes that de Blasio proposed in his short-lived candidacy for president, you had to add up all of Hillary's and Biden's proposed taxes and then double them to arrive at his $10 trillion in proposed taxes.[117]

While that was his vision on a national level, not the city level, it epitomizes his mindset and vision for society. Among the various tax hikes he proposed nationally was a top tax bracket of 70 percent—though if he continues getting his way, we'll reach a point where New York's high earners pay as much.

Tax hikes thus far have funded an ever-growing government. Following the great recession of 2008–2009, the number of full-time and full-time-equivalent workers for the city contracted nearly 6 percent from 311,018 in 2008 to 293,550 by 2012. By the end of 2019, there were 22,841 more employed by the city than the prior peak in 2008, with employment growing 36,510, from

---

116 Mairead McArdle, "De Blasio's Wife Employs Six Undisclosed Taxpayer-Funded Staffers: Report," *National Review,* August 18, 2020, https://www.nationalreview.com/news/de-blasios-wife-employs-six-undisclosed-taxpayer-funded-staffers-report/.

117 Tom Hebert, "Bill de Blasio Calls for $10 Trillion Tax Increase," Americans for Tax Reform, August 5, 2019, https://www.atr.org/bill-de-blasio-calls-10-trillion-tax-increase.

297,349 the year de Blasio took office to 333,859 by 2020.[118] For each new public employee hired, he further adds to the ticking time bomb that is their public pensions.

When de Blasio took office, the city was halfway through a fiscal year where it would spend $76.2 billion. By 2019, the annual budget increased 20.5 percent to $91.8 billion. Personal income tax revenues specifically amounted to $9.2 billion the year de Blasio was elected and increased by a third (after inflation) by 2019.[119]

As always, the problem is spending. The city's debt exploded from $39.5 billion in 2000 to $91.56 billion by 2019. Local tax revenues increased by 174 percent over the same time period.[120]

Overall, NYC ranks number one when it comes to local tax burdens in the U.S.[121] Things are still good for those in power, however, as de Blasio's property tax bill on his homes worth a combined $3.6 million in 2020 was $9,000.[122]

---

118 Maria Doulis, "The Growth of NYC Employee Headcount," Citizens Budget Commission, May 18, 2020, https://cbcny.org/research/growth-nyc-employee-headcount.

119 Nicole Gelinas, "What de Blasio Won't Tell Democrats: His Spending in NYC Is Killing the Middle Class," Manhattan Institute, August 5, 2019, https://www.manhattan-institute.org/de-blasio-spending-in-nyc-is-killing-the-middle-class.

120 Scott M. Stringer, New York City Comptroller, *Annual Report on Capital Debt and Obligations*, 2020, https://comptroller.nyc.gov/reports/annual-report-on-capital-debt-and-obligations/.

121 James Murphy, "Financial Crisis Looming for NYC as It Teeters on the Edge of Bankruptcy," *The New American*, March 12, 2019, https://www.thenewamerican.com/economy/economics/item/31714-financial-crisis-looming-for-nyc-as-it-teeters-on-the-edge-of-bankruptcy.

122 Matt Troutman, "Mayor to Pay Just $9K in Taxes on Homes Worth $3.6M: Records," Patch, February 14, 2020, https://patch.com/new-york/parkslope/mayor-pay-just-9k-taxes-homes-worth-3-6m-records.

Pensions

In 2019, New York City faced a nearly -$200 billion net position, 75 percent of which was due to pension and other retirement-related liabilities.[123] A city's net position, simply defined, is what it has left over after its debts are settled. Pensions play a large role in this.

Like many other cities facing pension difficulties, NYC has relied on optimistic projections of future market returns that never materialized. The New York City Employees Retirement System (NYCERS) and Teachers Retirement System (TRS) are the city's two largest and cover most public sector employees. They assumed rates of return of 8 percent from 2001–2012 and then 7 percent thereafter, whereas the actual returns those pensions received averaged roughly 6 percent during the period 2001–2017, the difference adding to the city's pension deficit.[124]

The funded ratio (fund assets divided by liabilities) for NYCERS is 71.4 percent (after being fully funded through 2004) and is 58.6 percent for TRS (which was fully funded through 2001).

These deficits come despite a massive rise in employer contribution rates into those funds. Employer contributions for NYCERS now compose 26 percent of payroll, and 44 percent for TRS.

---

123 Jen Sidorova, "New York City's Pension Debt Could Push It to Bankruptcy," Reason Foundation, May 16, 2019, https://reason.org/commentary/new-york-citys-pension-debt-is-driving-it-to-bankruptcy/.

124 Charles F. McElwee and Don Boyd, "Interview: Covid-19 and the Public-Pension Crisis," *City Journal*, April 25, 2020, https://www.city-journal.org/covid-19-and-the-public-pension-crisis.

Overall, pension liabilities make up 11 percent of the city's budget and consume 17 percent of its tax revenues.[125]

Escape from New York

If you're asking why anyone would want to live in New York in light of the information provided thus far, many New Yorkers are asking themselves the same question.

The number of citizens leaving the state is at its highest rate since NYC's pre-Giuliani crime wave. From 2010 to 2017, New York lost 1,022,071 residents, a negative 5.27 percent change in internal migration.[126] Total population grew only 0.4 percent from 2010 to 2019, at a time when the national population grew 16 percent.

NYC's population is beginning to drop for the first time in a decade. From 2017 to 2018, it fell 0.47 percent, which may appear minor but was the largest drop in any metro area during that period. While the population was projected to grow by seven thousand, it actually declined by thirty-eight thousand.[127] The exodus accelerated from 2018 to 2019, with the city losing over fifty-three thousand people.

During the early months of the pandemic, nearly half a million people left the city, though we won't know for some time how many left for good. Even immigrants are avoiding the city; international immigration fell nearly half since its peak in 2016 (far out of proportion with the decline in legal immigration under President Trump). By 2019, NYC's population was only 2

125 Sidorova.

126 Tate, 128.

127 Michelle Cohen, "Census Data Shows New York City's Population Has Been Shrinking for the First Time in Over a Decade," 6SQFT, April 18, 2019, https://www.6sqft.com/census-data-shows-new-york-citys-population-has-been-shrinking-for-the-first-time-in-over-a-decade/.

percent larger than it was in 2010,[128] again, a time period where the population grew 16 percent nationally.

The number one destination for those leaving New York is Florida,[129] a state that couldn't possibly contrast with New York more in terms of government size and scope. A comparison between the administration of both states leaves no doubt why a person would leave one for the other.

As the Cato Institute's Chris Edwards writes:

> New York and Florida have similar populations of 20 million and 21 million, respectively. But governments in New York spent twice as much as governments in Florida, $348 billion compared to $177 billion [in 2017].[130]

The two are similar only in spending on transportation, police, fire, parks, sewers, and sanitation. In other words, the kind of government spending no one has a problem with. Edwards continues, noting:

> New York spent $69 billion on K-12 schools in 2017 compared to Florida's $28 billion. Yet the states have about the same number of kids enrolled—2.7 million in New York and 2.8 million in Florida.

128 Michael Hendrix, "The End of Cities?" Economics21, March 31, 2020, https://economics21.org/have-we-reached-the-end-of-cities.

129 Joseph Spector, "New Yorkers Fleeing for Florida More Than Any Other State," *Democrat & Chronicle*, April 29, 2019, https://www.democratandchronicle.com/story/news/politics/albany/2019/04/29/new-yorkers-fleeing-florida-more-than-any-other-state/3616563002/.

130 Chris Edwards, "New York's Government Is Twice the Size of Florida's," Cato Institute, January 13, 2020, https://www.cato.org/blog/new-york-government-twice-size-floridas.

Despite that, the two rank similarly on a handful of rankings of educating. Florida ranks twenty-seventh on *U.S. News and World Report*'s education rankings to New York's twenty-fifth.[131]

Florida has an average SAT score of 999 to New York's 1,064, but this discrepancy in New York's favor is due to sampling bias. Florida has nearly all students take the test, while only 79 percent of New York students take it.[132] When a group that likely places in the bottom fifth in terms of academic performance doesn't take a test, the results are obviously going to present a rosier picture than exists in reality.

While graduation rates are similar between the two states (86 percent in New York vs. 88 percent in Florida), only nine schools in the entire state of New York have a 100 percent graduation rate (of 1,217 ranked schools), while Florida has forty-one (of 598 ranked schools).[133]

On welfare, Edwards notes:

New York spent $71 billion on public welfare compared to Florida's $28 billion. Liberals say that governments provide needed resources to people truly in need. Conservatives say that generous handouts induce high demand whether people need it or not. Given that New

---

131 Brett Ziegler, "Education Rankings: Measuring How Well States Are Educating Their Students," *USNews*, 2020, https://www.usnews.com/news/best-states/rankings/education.

132 Allen Cheng, "Average SAT Scores by State," PrepScholar, October 6, 2019, https://blog.prepscholar.com/average-sat-scores-by-state-most-recent.

133 Emma Kerr and Melissa Shin, "See High School Graduation Rates by State," *USNews*, April 22, 2020, https://www.usnews.com/education/best-high-schools/articles/see-high-school-graduation-rates-by-state.

York's welfare costs are 2.5 times higher than Florida's, the latter effect probably dominates.

New York's welfare benefits are on par with those of a European social democracy. According to Michael Tanner, "In New York, a mother with two children under the age of five who participates in six major welfare programs (Temporary Assistance for Needy Families, Supplemental Nutrition Assistance Program, housing assistance, the Low Income Home Energy Assistance Program, the Special Supplemental Nutrition Program for Women, Infants, and Children and free commodities would receive a total benefits package with a value of more than $27,500 per year."

A mother would be entitled to $17,324 in France, $23,257 in Germany, and $22,211 in Sweden. This comparison doesn't include Medicaid (which would be worth $10,560 to the U.S. household) because Europe's health care systems aren't targeted exclusively to the poor (or elderly).[134]

Tanner also notes that New York does a poor job of enforcing restrictions on state welfare. "A recent government report found that New York had almost 11,000 families with income over the statutory limit still living in public housing, by far the most in the nation; one family earning almost $500,000 continued to receive assistance."

Despite Florida being a known retirement destination, according to Edwards:

Retirement systems are mainly funded by contributions and investment earnings, although most systems are underfunded. New York has a larger and more unionized

---

134 Michael D. Tanner, "New York Welfare: More Generous Than Sweden or France," Cato Institute, August 26, 2015, https://www.cato.org/publications/commentary/new-york-welfare-more-generous-sweden-or-france.

public workforce than Florida. New York governments employed 1,196,632 workers in 2017 compared to Florida's 889,950 (measured in FTEs). New York's public workforce is 67 percent unionized compared to Florida's at 27 percent.

And as a result of all that inefficient spending, New York spends $10 billion more annually on interest costs than Florida.

Despite the dearth of reasons anyone would want to live in New York, Cuomo blames President Trump for the exodus of citizens and the fiscal problems that have compounded for the state.

Upon announcing an unexpected $2.3 billion budget shortfall in February 2019, Cuomo said that the capping of state and local tax deductions people are allowed to write off resulting from Trump's tax bill helped expedite the rate of people leaving the state.[135] While that's obviously added to the list of reasons people are leaving, there were plenty of others before the Trump tax cuts (as this chapter clearly shows). What Cuomo is really complaining about is that he can't raise taxes and have the rest of the country subsidize it by giving them federal write-offs. Or in other words, Cuomo is acknowledging that people don't want to live in his state when they have to pay the full cost of it.

After all, if Cuomo wanted to retain citizens, he could simply not tax them as much and enable that by reducing the size of government. Not coincidentally, states with the highest spending on welfare also have the highest out-migration rates. New York leads the pack, followed by Connecticut, California, Massachusetts, and Illinois.[136]

---

135 Tate, 12.

136 Tate, 9.

It is generally middle- and higher-income taxpayers leaving, creating a death spiral where high social spending requires high taxes alongside a shrinking tax base, increasing the demand for even higher taxes on those who remain. Without the rich, those taxes tend to be regressive. Just one example of that is red light cameras, as evidenced by the states with the highest concentration of red light cameras including the highly indebted blue states New York, California, Maryland, Illinois, and the District of Columbia. New York also tops the list of states with the most tolls.[137]

Additionally, New York has:

- The seventh highest gas tax at 45.9 cents per gallon.[138]
- The twenty-second highest liquor tax at $6.44 per gallon of spirits.[139]
- The tenth highest state sales tax at 8.52 percent, and the fourth highest average local sales tax rate at 4.52 percent.[140]
- The fourth highest property taxes at $2,782 per capita.[141]

Income tax rates range from 4 percent on income below $8,501 to 8.82 percent on income above $1,077,550 (as of 2020),[142]

137 Tate, 23.

138 Janelle Cammenga, "State Gasoline Tax Rates as of July 2019," Tax Foundation, July 31, 2019, https://taxfoundation.org/state-gas-tax-rates-2019/.

139 Morgan Scarboro, "How High Are Spirits Taxes in Your State?" Tax Foundation, March 22, 2018, https://taxfoundation.org/state-spirits-taxes-2018/.

140 Janelle Cammenga, "State and Local Sales Tax Rates, 2020," Tax Foundation, January 15, 2020, https://taxfoundation.org/2020-sales-taxes/.

141 Katherine Loughead, "How Much Does Your State Collect in Property Taxes Per Capita?" Tax Foundation, March 13, 2019, https://taxfoundation.org/property-taxes-per-capita-2019/.

142 "Tax Year 2019 New York Income Tax Brackets," Tax-Brackets.org, 2020, https://www.tax-brackets.org/newyorktaxtable.

and total income taxes paid per person are up over 50 percent since 2010 alone.[143]

Property taxes in particular have been destructive to small business in the city. NYC's retail store buildings paid a total of $1.5 billion in property taxes in 2018, a 72 percent increase from 2009. Property taxes in office and residential buildings increased 69 percent and 66 percent, respectively. The average property tax paid by the average small merchant increased from $46,620 to $78,954.[144]

As is the case with regulation, any cost imposed on businesses will disproportionately impact small businesses, which are, to borrow the most popular cliché among politicians, the "city's backbone." Of over two hundred thousand businesses in NYC, 98 percent are small (fewer than one hundred employees) and 89 percent are "very small" (fewer than twenty employees). In total, they employ half of the city.[145]

"The Worst Place to Do Business in America"

As you've gleaned from the chapter documenting the coronavirus response from New York City and the state as a whole, liberal incompetence proved fatal.

The default economic illiteracy of liberal leaders remained intact during the pandemic, leading to them making everything worse for the living. The states that saw both the most coronavirus

---

143 "State Government Tax Collections, Total Income Taxes in New York," FRED, May 1, 2020, https://fred.stlouisfed.org/series/NYTLINCTAX.

144 Gene Marks, "Mayor de Blasio, the Small Business Killer," The Hill, August 22, 2019, https://thehill.com/opinion/finance/458343-mayor-de-blasio-the-small-business-killer.

145 "Small Business First," City of New York, 2020, https://www1.nyc.gov/assets/smallbizfirst/downloads/pdf/small-business-first-report.pdf.

deaths per capita and highest increases in unemployment were blue states.[146]

National retailers such as Shake Shack, Applebee's, Lids, and others said that their stores are recovering slower in NYC (Manhattan specifically) than anywhere else in the country. That includes even New Jersey, the one state hit harder by the virus than New York.

Shake Shack's 58 percent decline in NYC sales by the middle of the year was its worst decline among all its regions. Lids saw its foot traffic at its best performing stores in NY (which are located in NYC) decline 85 percent over the past year, compared to 20 percent at its other stores.[147]

The extent to which the economic damage during the coronavirus is weighted between the virus itself and the lockdowns is still debated, but regardless, New York saw the worst of both worlds, having imposed a strict lockdown (far too late, it seems) and being among the states hardest hit by the virus. Not only that, its lockdowns continue even as the state goes days without a single coronavirus death.

The nonprofit Partnership for New York City, which consists of a select group of nearly three hundred CEOs from NYC's top firms, released a depressing "post pandemic" report estimating the permanent damage the lockdowns will have for businesses. The report, aided by twelve global consulting firms, found that a third of the city's 230,000 small businesses may never reopen.

---

146 Matt Palumbo, "Blue States Lead the Nation in Unemployment," *Dan Bongino Show*, August 25, 2020, https://bongino.com/blue-states-lead-the-nation-in-unemployment.

147 Lisa Fickensher, "NYC Is Now the Worst Place to Do Business, Retailers Say," *New York Post,* July 21, 2020, https://nypost.com/2020/07/21/nyc-is-now-the-worst-place-to-do-business-retailers-say/.

The report found that before the pandemic, most businesses had less than three months' worth of cash reserves, which was roughly how long the lockdowns had been going on at the time of the release of the report (July 2020). "That means that funds to restart, pay back rent and buy inventory are exhausted, leaving tens of thousands of entrepreneurs at risk, particularly business owners of color," according to the report.[148]

It would later be learned in August that 83 percent of NYC's restaurants were unable to pay their July rent.[149] Some made partial payments, but 37 percent paid no rent at all.

Among the other bleak findings from the Partnership for New York City report were that:

By June, NYC "experienced more infection, death and economic destruction than anywhere in the world."

Up to eighty thousand of the city's small businesses "may never reopen."

The unemployment rate was 18.3 percent and one million are struggling.

Only 40 percent of Manhattan office workers will return by year's end and 25 percent may never come back. This is likely to have ripple effects, damaging those who own office space.

---

148 "A Call for Action and Collaboration," Partnership for New York City, 2020, https://pfnyc.org/wp-content/uploads/2020/07/actionandcollaboration. pdf.

149 Tyler Durden, "'Financially Devastated'—83% of NYC Restaurants Unable to Pay July Rent," ZeroHedge, August 10, 2020, https://www.zerohedge.com/markets/financially-devastated-83-nyc-restaurants-unable-pay-july-rent.

The city's economy is projected to shrink 7 percent, which will further reduce the tax base. Outward migration will compound this problem.[150]

Everyone had thought that the relatively wealthy four hundred thousand–plus who left the city at the beginning of the pandemic would simply return in a month or two. For the large part that has yet to materialize, as evidenced by apartment vacancies reaching record highs alongside falling rents. Many have been able to work from home, and others can see the visible decay that has materialized at an alarming rate in the city they had fled. As Fox Business's Charles Gasparino puts it: "Wall Street could soon become a home office and a computer."

Even by the end of August, when the rest of the state had already brought indoor dining back at half capacity for two and a half months, de Blasio didn't have a care in the world for the city's restaurants. "Indoor dining, that's not a plan right now," he told radio host Brian Lehrer. "There's not a context for indoor dining. We're never saying it's impossible. But we do not, based on what we're seeing around the world, we do not have a plan for reopening indoor dining in the near term."[151]

Days later de Blasio was asked an obvious question: Why would indoor dining be banned when schools would be allowing

---

150 *Post* Editorial Board. "NYC's Elected Leaders Haven't Begun to Face Its Economic and Fiscal Horrors," *New York Post,* July 25, 2020, https:// nypost.com/2020/07/25/nycs-elected-leaders-havent-begun-to-face-its-economic-and-fiscal-horrors/.

151 Julia Marsh, "De Blasio Has 'No Plan' for Return of Indoor Dining in NYC," *New York Post,* August 21, 2020, https://nypost.com/2020/ 08/21/de-blasio-has-no-plan-for-return-of-indoor-dining-in-nyc/.

children to eat inside at lunch tables when the school year begins? "I don't think there's a similarity at all," de Blasio replied.[152]

Real estate developer and Democrat donor Don Peebles, whose firm is based in lower Manhattan, told CNBC: "I think it's going to take New York about a decade or so to dig out of this. Maybe longer. But it's not going to be soon."[153]

Things are looking bad, but de Blasio at least hasn't resorted to begging them to stay—yet.

Cuomo Begs People to Stop Leaving—and for a Bailout

Andrew Cuomo finally woke up to the fact that high taxes on the wealthy are driving them out of his state during the coronavirus pandemic.

Speaking at a press conference in August, Cuomo addressed the wealthiest residents who left NYC. "I literally talk to people all day long who are in their Hamptons house who also lived here, or in their Hudson Valley house or in their Connecticut weekend house, and I say, 'You gotta come back, when are you coming back?'"

"We'll go to dinner, I'll buy you a drink. Come over, I'll cook," the sales pitch continued.

"They're not coming back right now. And you know what else they're thinking? If I stay there, I pay a lower income tax because they don't pay the New York City surcharge."

---

152 Julia Marsh and Lia Eustachewich, "De Blasio's Tale of 2 Brunches: Mayor Has No Plan for 'Optional' Indoor Dining," *New York Post*, August 25, 2020, https://nypost.com/2020/08/25/nyc-has-no-concrete-plan-to-return-indoor-dining-de-blasio/.

153 "New York May Take a Decade to Recover from Coronavirus Pandemic, Says Developer Don Peebles," CNBC, August 21, 2020, https://www.cnbc.com/2020/08/21/don-peebles-new-york-city-may-take-decade-to-recover-from-coronavirus.html.

New York does need to retain its wealthy to survive, but for the reasons outlined in this book, it's going to take more than dinner and a drink.[154]

Meanwhile, he wants the fiscal cost of the pandemic paid for by everyone outside his state.

While countless firms were being bailed out during the pandemic, Cuomo attempted to make the case that his debt-ridden state deserved one too. That came after President Trump spoke out against the idea, telling the *New York Post*, "It's not fair to the Republicans because all the states that need help—they're run by Democrats in every case. Florida is doing phenomenal, Texas is doing phenomenal, the Midwest is, you know, fantastic—very little debt."

Trump also said, "You look at Illinois, you look at New York, look at California, you know, those three, there's tremendous debt there, and many others. I don't think the Republicans want to be in a position where they bail out states that are, that have been mismanaged over a long period of time."

Cuomo fired back, arguing that bailing out a state like his would simply be a return of money they paid to the federal government. As he argued, New York pays $29 billion more to the federal government than they get back.[155]

---

154 Jennifer Smith, "Cuomo Begs Wealthy New Yorkers to Come Back to Save the City and Pleads 'I'll Buy You a Drink!' as He Fights Off Calls to Raise Their Taxes—Which He Fears May Scare Them Away Forever," *Daily Mail,* August 5, 2020, https://www.dailymail.co.uk/news/article-8595717/Cuomo-begs-wealthy-New-Yorkers-come-save-city-Ill-buy-drink.html.

155 @GannettAlbany, "You want to be fair, just give back the money to New York you took," Cuomo says. "Who gives and who takes? We know the facts and the numbers," Twitter, May 5, 2020, 11:02 a.m., https://twitter.com/GannettAlbany/status/1257702228984360962.

And he is correct (to some extent)—New York is one among just seven states that send more to the federal government each year than they receive back. In New York's case it's due to having fewer federal employees than other states and higher than average nominal incomes (leading to them paying a third more taxes per capita than other states). According to a report from the Office of the New York State Comptroller, the amount of funds the state receives for services is in line with other states:[156]

- New York received $138.1 billion in direct payments including those to individuals who receive Social Security, Medicare, benefits for veterans and retired federal employees, and food assistance, which was close to the average among states on a per capita basis. Major programs for which the state received higher-than-average per capita expenditures include Medicare, food assistance, and Supplemental Security Income.

- New York was second in the country in grants to state and local governments, receiving $69.8 billion. Medicaid makes up more than half of all federal spending for such grants, and the state's per capita Medicaid funding from Washington ranked first among all states.

- Federal salaries and benefits are also being counted in these statistics. In two other major categories—procurement and federal employee compensation—federal spending in New York was less than half of the national

---

156 "New York Continues to Send More Federal Tax Dollars to Washington Than It Gets in Return," Office of the New York State Comptroller, January 14, 2020, https://www.osc.state.ny.us/press/releases/2020/01/new-york-continues-send-more-federal-tax-dollars-washington-it-gets-return?redirect=legacy.

average on a per capita basis. The state's combined total, $19.3 billion, was 2.5 percent of the nationwide total.

If procurement and federal employee compensation were on par with other states, New York would still be a net taxpayer, albeit to a lesser extent (of roughly $10 billion). The rest of the gap is due to the fact that New York is home to a city with more millionaires than any other in the world (for now).[157]

In other words, New York as a state is a net taxpayer because millionaires don't get welfare too. I guess Cuomo didn't think his argument would sound as convincing if he put it that way.

And while New York receives less than it puts in, it still already receives more back from the federal government than the average state on a per capita basis relative to other states. The average state receives $6,135 in federal spending per citizen—while New York receives $8,384.[158]

And all that aside, it doesn't change the fact that New York has racked up over $136 billion in debt, and that doesn't include $65 billion in off balance sheet liabilities. In fact, that they racked up this much debt when they have a tax base that is far wealthier than the rest of the country should be yet another reason against the rest of us bailing them out.[159]

---

157 Kathleen Elkins, "New York City Is Home to Nearly 1 Million Millionaires, More Than Any Other City in the World," CNBC, January 18, 2019, https://www.cnbc.com/2019/01/18/new-york-city-has-more-millionaires-than-any-other-city-in-the-world.html.

158 "Total State Expenditures per Capita," Kaiser Family Foundation, August 3, 2020, https://www.kff.org/other/state-indicator/per-capita-state-spending.

159 *Financial State of the States: An Annual Report by Truth in Accounting,* Truth in Accounting, September 2019, https://www.truthinaccounting.org/library/doclib/FSOS-booklet-2019.pdf.

NEW YORK CITY'S WAR ON EDUCATION

New York City's schools are failing, and Bill de Blasio has adamantly condemned the one solution we know for sure works: choice.

De Blasio has launched a war against his city's charter schools. "I hate the privatizers and I want to stop them," he told teachers at a union-sponsored education forum in July 2019. "I am angry about the privatizers. I am sick and tired of these efforts to privatize a precious thing we need—public education. I know we're not supposed to be saying 'hate'—our teachers taught us not to—I hate the privatizers and I want to stop them," he said, unaware the charter schools aren't private schools. "Get away from high-stakes testing, get away from charter schools. No federal funding for charter schools," he said.[160]

With opposition like that, you'd assume that the evidence against charter schools was overwhelming, yet the evidence is overwhelming only in proving the opposite.

To start with some context, the National Assessment of Educational Progress test (effectively the "national report card" on the performance of fourth and eighth graders in math, reading, and other subjects) shows that only 32 percent of NYC's fourth graders in public schools are proficient in math, 27 percent in reading, and 18 percent in science. For eighth graders, the figures are 27 percent for math, 26 percent for reading, and 13 percent for science.[161] All these proficiency rates lag the national average for public schools, and large city public schools specifically (though they all have much room for improvement).

---

160 Julia Marsh, "De Blasio Shouts That He 'Hates' Charter Schools at Campaign Event," *New York Post*, July 8, 2019, https://nypost.com/2019/07/08/de-blasio-shouts-that-he-hates-charter-schools-at-campaign-event/.

161 "How Did U.S. Students Perform on the Most Recent Assessments?," The Nation's Report Card, 2020, https://www.nationsreportcard.gov/.

With test scores like New York City's, one might think a mayor would be desperate to try anything to improve them, even if it meant trying something completely new. You'd never expect opposition to the solution we already know works from a mountain of evidence: charter schools.

As a result of the New York Charter Schools Act of 1998, there are now almost three hundred charter schools in New York State. According to a 2017 study on Charter Performance in New York (the entirety of the state, not just NYC) published by Stanford University's Center for Research on Education Outcome:

> The analysis shows that in a year's time, the typical charter school student in New York shows stronger growth in both reading and math compared to the educational gains that the students would have had in a traditional public school (TPS). The findings are statistically significant for both reading and math.
>
> **Thinking of a 180-day school year as "one year of learning," an average New York charter student demonstrates stronger growth equivalent to completing 34 additional days of learning in reading and 63 additional days of learning in math in a year's time.** [emphasis mine] Probing these overall findings, the analysis reveals that certain subgroups exhibit stronger growth than their TPS peers while others do not. Notable growth occurs among Hispanic and Black charter students in poverty, who post stronger growth compared to their counterparts in TPS, during the period of the study.

Overall, over the four growth periods of the study, charter students demonstrate positive growth in both reading and math.[162]

Of NYC in particular, a NY1 education report by Jillian Jorgensen notes:

> While Mayor Bill Blasio touted gains in test scores by public school students that were announced Thursday, their peers in charter schools are still doing better: 63 percent of the charter students in grades 3 through 8 passed the state math exam this year, compared to 46 percent in traditional public schools. And 57 percent of charter students were proficient in English Language Arts, compared to 47 percent in regular public schools.[163]

As Jorgensen alluded to, de Blasio was quick to point out that test scores increased among non-charter public schools, and he even went as far as to credit his $500 million–plus per year "universal pre-kindergarten" policy for that.

If extra spending is what caused the minuscule increase in test scores de Blasio boasts about, then what explains charter school's superior performance despite inferior funding per student? NYC's charters are the least funded in the city, receiving

---

162 "Charter School Performance in New York," CREDO, September 2017, https://credo.stanford.edu/sites/g/files/sbiybj6481/f/ny_state_report_2017_06_01_final.pdf.

163 Jillian Jorgensen, "A Look at How NY Charters Performed on State Tests Compared to Public Schools," Spectrum News NY 1, August 23, 2019, https://www.ny1.com/nyc/all-boroughs/news/2019/08/23/2019-new-york-test-scores-charter-school-students-compared-to-public-school-students.

20 percent (about $5,000) less than their traditional public-school counterparts.[164]

Cuomo deserves some credit for siding with sanity on the charter school issue, publicly declaring his support for them in 2014. "We know that too many public schools are failing. [There are] over 200 failing schools, [a] 6% grade level for reading, 5% grade level for math. We need new ideas. Einstein said insanity is doing the same thing over and over and over again and expecting a different result," he said.[165]

While Einstein never actually said that (probably in part because he had access to a dictionary), Cuomo is otherwise correct.

NYC's Elite Schools

Opposition to charters is just the tip of the iceberg when it comes to de Blasio's war against the few parts of his city's education system that work. Another subject of his ire has been the city's elite schools (Stuyvesant, Bronx Science, Brooklyn Tech, and six others), with his criticism centering on their disproportionate composition of Asian and white students, while few blacks and Hispanics attend such schools.

Of Stuyvesant's fall 2019 freshman class, only seven of 895 are African American, while three-quarters of the class is Asian American. Across all the elite schools, just over 10 percent of

---

164 David Cantor, "NYC Charter Schools Get 20% Less Funding Than Traditional Schools, Study Says," The 74 Million, August 30, 2017, https://www.the74million.org/article/nyc-charter-schools-get-20-less-funding-than-traditional-schools-study-says/.

165 Kimberlee Payton-Jones, "Cuomo Reiterates Support for Charter Schools," American School & University, March 5, 2014, https://www.asumag.com/dailynews/article/20851598/cuomo-reiterates-support-for-charter-schools.

students are black and Hispanic but account for 70 percent of the city's school enrollment.[166]

Leftists are skilled at selectively caring about statistical over- and underrepresentation. Can you imagine a single progressive pretending that it's an injustice that white men are overrepresented as garbage collectors? Of course not, but when a similar overrepresentation appears in a desirable field (or in this case, school) they will immediately make allegations that racism is behind the discrepancy. Furthermore, while progressives will often talk about the need for more representation from minorities or "people of color," Asians seem to have been randomly removed from that demographic.

De Blasio argues that NYC's elite schools amount to segregation because they have standards. "People want to see change. That's why we're doing something bold here, and we're saying we're not going to live by this old system that has perpetuated massive segregation—not just segregation, massive segregation."

We've indeed come a long way from the days of Jim Crow when "segregation" is now synonymous with a test that anyone in the city can study for and take.

To fix this nonexistent problem he's diagnosed, de Blasio unsuccessfully attempted to end entrance exams to elite schools so they wouldn't be able to determine which elite students to admit. For eight of the nine elite schools, admission is determined solely by the Specialized High Schools Admissions Test. Students are admitted in rank order starting with those with the highest scores.

---

166 Alex Zimmerman, "De Blasio Decries 'Segregation' amid Specialized High School Debate—a Term He Has Avoided," Chalkbeat New York, March 22, 2019, https://ny.chalkbeat.org/2019/3/22/21107113/de-blasio-decries-segregation-amid-specialized-high-school-debate-a-term-he-has-avoided.

De Blasio instead wanted to have these elite schools admit the top 7 percent of every middle school class, a move that de Blasio's administration says could boost black and Hispanic enrollment by as much as 45 percent.[167] While that's huge in terms of a percentage, in context it would imply that the current system would be uprooted so that Stuyvesant's next freshman class would have roughly three extra black students.

Fortunately, de Blasio's proposal failed, but this whole ordeal serves as a reminder that de Blasio weighs equal outcomes over equal opportunity.

Gifted and Talented Programs

While a lack of his preferred type of diversity at schools is a problem in the eyes of de Blasio, so is the best performing students being minorities (so long as they are Asian). His School Diversity Advisory Group (SDAG) came out with a set of recommendations aimed at "desegregating" his city's public schools. Among the proposals was the abolition of gifted and talented programs, and the equally insane suggestion they eliminate all criteria of student performance.

According to the SDAG, gifted and talented programs are but the latest example of institutional racism (what isn't?). "While Brown vs. Board of Education mandated school integration in 1954, gifted programs were used as a method of avoiding required integration. A wave of new gifted programs were founded in the 1970s...This wave also coincided with a number of national

---

167 Christina Veiga, "What's Happened in the Year Since Mayor Bill de Blasio Called for Overhauling NYC's Specialized High School Admissions," Chalkbeat New York, June 1, 2019, https://ny.chalkbeat. org/2019/6/1/21108237/what-s-happened-in-the-year-since-mayor-bill-de-blasio-called-for-overhauling-nyc-s-specialized-high.

resegregation efforts, which used anti-school busing legislation and other tactics to clandestinely reinstitute separated schools," the report reads.[168]

None of that is true, of course. But in character, de Blasio seconds the recommended insanity. Following the report, he floated abolishing tests for four-year-olds to enter his city's gifted and talented program. When asked by WNYC radio host Brian Lehrer if he'd eliminate those tests, de Blasio responded, "That could be part of the process, I think it's a great question."

De Blasio continued, indicating that his main problem is with excellence itself: "If we think of isolating a small group of kids and calling them gifted and talented and then leaving a whole bunch of other kids without the opportunity to display their gifts and have them supported, something's wrong there."[169]

He said he'd take a year before making any changes, however.

At least one school did take initiative and do away with its program. Brooklyn's Public School 9 is 40 percent black, 31 percent white, 17 percent Hispanic, and 9 percent Asian, but still voluntarily ended its gifted and talented program for incoming kindergartners because the majority of those taking part in it are white and Asian.[170]

---

168 Matt Welch, "De Blasio Advisory Group Wants to Abolish Gifted Classes in NYC Public Schools," *Reason,* August 28, 2019, https://reason. com/2019/08/28/de-blasio-advisory-group-wants-to-abolish-gifted-classes-in-nyc-public-schools/.

169 Julia Marsh and Selim Algar, "De Blasio: I May Scrap Gifted and Talented Testing for 4-Year-Olds," *New York Post,* September 6, 2019, https://nypost.com/2019/09/06/de-blasio-i-may-scrap-gifted-and-talented-testing-for-4-year-olds/.

170 Erin Richards, "New York Is in Uproar over Push to Ax Gifted Programs. This School Is Doing It Anyway," *USA Today,* January 13, 2020, https:// www.usatoday.com/story/news/education/2020/01/13/nyc-doe-racist-segregation-brooklyn-specialized-high-school-exam-gifted/2763549001/.

It must be stated that so long as any system of education differs from traditional public education, de Blasio is against it, and he'll find any excuse to justify his stance. While the crux of his argument against elite schools has been the underrepresentation of blacks and Hispanics, this is just his Trojan Horse. De Blasio either ignores or is ignorant of the overrepresentation of black and Hispanic students in outperforming charter schools—which he also opposes.

As the Manhattan Institute notes:

> [Charter schools] now educate 123,000 students, or 10% of all public school students in the city, in 236 schools. Minority students from impoverished families benefit most from New York City's charter schools, which offer strong academics and the prospect of upward mobility. Over 80% of charter students are low-income, and 91% are African-American or Hispanic.[171]

Perhaps diversity isn't actually what de Blasio is concerned with, but anything that conflicts with his liberal vision that everyone should receive an equal (but terrible) education in government schools.

Failing Schools

During the reign of Michael Bloomberg, over 150 failing schools were closed and replaced with over two hundred smaller, more innovative schools. Graduation rates at the closed schools were below 40 percent, but the graduation rates of the students who

---

171 Ray Domanico, "Lift the Cap: Why New York City Needs More Charter Schools," Manhattan Institute, February 20, 2019, https://www.manhattan-institute.org/nyc-charter-school-benefits-over-public-schools.

would have otherwise attended them and didn't, had graduation rates fifteen percentage points higher at their new schools.[172]

While this was a success, de Blasio's solution to failing schools became his signature educational initiative, "Renewal Schools." Like a gambling addict, de Blasio used the program to chase his losses and dump hundreds of millions into failing schools.

After four years and $774 million, the program ended after making no meaningful impact.[173] One of the takeaways is that many failing schools are indeed beyond redemption, and it makes no sense to continuously plow more resources into schools that consistently fail year over year.

But it's not like de Blasio learned anything from this ordeal. "I am convinced it was the right road to go down," de Blasio said at a press conference after ending the program. "We did not say everything would be perfect."[174]

Indeed, it looks like nothing was perfect.

---

172 James J. Kemple, "High School Closures in New York City," NYU: The Research Alliance for New York City Schools, 2015, https://research. steinhardt.nyu.edu/research_alliance/publications/hs_closures_in_nyc.

173 Marcus A. Winters, "De Blasio's Renewal Fiasco Proves Bloomberg's Answer to Failed Schools Was Best for Kids," Manhattan Institute, February 28, 2019, https://www.manhattan-institute.org/html/ de-blasio-renewal-schools-fiasco-proves-bloomberg.

174 Alex Zimmerman, "New York City Ends Controversial Renewal Turnaround Program—but the Approach Is Here to Stay," Chalkbeat New York, February 26, 2019, https://ny.chalkbeat.org/2019/2/26/21106894/ new-york-city-ends-controversial-renewal-turnaround-program-but-the-approach-is-here-to-stay.

LAW AND ORDER IN NEW YORK CITY

Beginning in the 1960s, New York City underwent a great decivilization to which the city now risks returning.

Now the center of the world, the Times Square of the '60s through early '90s personified the city's failure as its red light district. Still lingering from the scars of the Great Depression, industrial decline, white flight, and most importantly the abandonment of law and order, the modern tourist trap descended into hedonism.

Before becoming home to Broadway, TV studios, and Disney, Times Square was home to the twenty-five-cent peep show, the Mafia, strip clubs, street prostitution, illicit gambling, and open-air drug markets.

By the late 1970s, the Times Square area recorded more felony and crime complaints than any other part of the city.[175] The Council of Public Safety released a pamphlet titled *Welcome to Fear City: A Survival Guide for Visitors to the City of New York*, which, among other advice, advised tourists not to walk, to avoid public transportation, and to stay off the streets after 6 p.m. Negative publicity ended up halting the distribution of the pamphlet.[176]

While Times Square was the epicenter, it served as the embodiment of what was happening city wide, with an estimated forty thousand prostitutes walking the streets throughout the 1970s. Nearly every single subway car was littered with graffiti. The welfare rolls exploded alongside public homelessness. One couldn't drive without being harassed for cash by a squeegee man.

Social decay created an environment ripe for violence. The city saw 1,814 homicides in 1980, roughly triple the number in the 2010s. Over the course of the previous decade, the city's population had declined by a million to just over seven million.[177]

Violence saw no signs of slowing down in the 1980s and peaked by 1990 with 2,245 murders. Groups like the Guardian Angels sprang up to combat the violence that the police weren't equipped or allowed to.

---

175 "From Dazzling to Dirty and Back Again: A Brief History of Times Square," Times Square Official Website, https://www.timessquarenyc.org/history-of-times-square.

176 Jen Carlson, "The 1970s Pamphlet Aimed at Keeping Tourists out of NYC," Gothamist, September 16, 2013, https://gothamist.com/arts-entertainment/the-1970s-pamphlet-aimed-at-keeping-tourists-out-of-nyc.

177 Christina Sterbenz, "New York City Used to Be a Terrifying Place," Business Insider, July 12, 2013, https://www.businessinsider.com/new-york-city-used-to-be-a-terrifying-place-photos-2013-7.

It wasn't until Rudy Giuliani took over as mayor and began cleaning up the city that things turned around. Total crime fell 64 percent during the Giuliani years, and murder fell 67 percent from 1,960 in Dinkins's last year (1993) to 640 in Giuliani's. That was more than the national drop in crime and in murders over that period. NYC's crime decline continued even when crime rose nationally.

Michael Bloomberg largely sustained Giuliani's legacy, and its effects even continued during the early years of Mayor Bill de Blasio's tenure. But the current mayor's recent reversals, if left unchecked, will usher in a decline from which the city may not ever recover.

A HISTORY OF LAW AND ORDER IN NEW YORK CITY

The problems Giuliani is credited with fixing were directly fueled by the policies of his predecessor, David Dinkins (and before him, Mayors Ed Koch, Abraham Beame, and John Lindsay).

The city had 2,263 murders during Dinkins' first year in office, but he assured the public that the police made no difference. Dinkins held the philosophy of so many liberals today, that you can't combat crime without combating the "root causes" of crime. "If we had a police officer on every corner, we couldn't stop some of the random violence that goes on," he said, blaming poverty and racism for crime. Still no word on why racism would cause crime, considering that most crime victims are victimized by someone of the same race.

Dinkins's solution was one that has resurged in popularity today—turning the police into social workers. His police commissioner Lee Brown agreed, and believed that instead of reacting to crime, police become "neighborhood problem solvers."

As violence continued to ravage the city, an iconic headline in the *New York Post* pleaded: "Dave, Do Something."

Unfortunately, Dinkins's "something" wasn't anything that would solve the problems he exacerbated with liberal policies that were cartoonish at best.

Giuliani recognized that crime isn't something inevitable, but a problem that can be solved. And to do so he implemented a new approach to policing alongside a massive increase in the city's police force.

If we were to classify crimes in a sort of Maslow's hierarchy with petty crime on the bottom and serious crimes on top, Giuliani saw combating petty crimes as essential to preventing more serious crimes, because a society that tolerates the former is more likely to tolerate the latter.

Underpinning Giuliani's philosophy on crime was the "broken-windows theory," advocated by criminologist James Q. Wilson. Wilson penned an influential 1982 article in *The Atlantic* in which he noted the following:

Philip Zimbardo, a Stanford psychologist, reported in 1969 on some experiments testing the broken-window theory. He arranged to have an automobile without license plates parked with its hood up on a street in the Bronx and a comparable automobile on a street in Palo Alto, California. The car in the Bronx was attacked by "vandals" within ten minutes of its "abandonment." The first to arrive were a family—father, mother, and young son—who removed the radiator and battery. Within twenty-four hours, virtually everything of value had been removed. Then random destruction began—windows were smashed, parts torn off, upholstery ripped. Children began to use the car as a playground. Most of the adult "vandals" were well-dressed, apparently clean-cut whites. The car in Palo Alto sat untouched for more than a week. Then Zimbardo smashed part of it with a sledgehammer. Soon, passersby were joining in. Within a few hours, the car had been turned upside down and utterly destroyed. Again, the "vandals" appeared to be primarily respectable whites.[178]

Giuliani echoed the theory: "Murder and graffiti are two vastly different crimes. But they are part of the same continuum, and a climate that tolerates one is more likely to tolerate the other." NYC's climate under Dinkins was one that tolerated every kind of broken window one could imagine: squeegee men, prostitution, vandalism, open-air drug markets, and more.

Giuliani changed the mission of the police to what common sense would suggest its purpose is: preventing crime in addition to responding to crimes when they do occur. NYPD police chief William Bratton reorganized the force and created a street crimes unit that flooded high crime areas and got illegal guns off the street. The NYPD's schedule also changed to 24/7, while previously most detectives and narcotics officers went off duty as 5 p.m. One of the most well-established findings in criminology (besides a greater police presence leading to less crime) is that most crimes occur at night.

The city began compiling a database known as CompStat to track crime patterns in the city and more efficiently mobilize officers to respond in those areas.

Bratton replaced a third of the city's seventy-six precinct commanders in only a few months, demanding results. Giuliani analogized the performance of different precincts to a bank with

---

178 George L. Kelling and James Q. Wilson, "Broken Windows: The Police and Neighborhood Safety," *The Atlantic*, March 1982, https://www.theatlantic.com/magazine/archive/1982/03/broken-windows/304465/.

seventy-six branches; that an underperforming branch would require changes in operations (in this case, in leadership).

Liberals made the clichéd response to Giuliani's policies that are unavoidable today: that any reduction in crime must be understood against the backdrop of racial bias in policing.

These kinds of arguments are always based on individual cases and provide no context to the greater picture. So long as we live in a country with hundreds of millions of people, improbable tragedies are an inevitability, but that doesn't indicate a trend. Nor is there ever any acknowledgment of trends improving. As tens of millions marched nationwide following the death of George Floyd, this came following a year that represented an 80 percent decline in the number of unarmed black men killed by police since 2015.

In Giuliani's case, critics focused on the killings of unarmed black men Amadou Diallo and Patrick Dorismond. This occurred during a time period (1995–2000) when civilian complaints of excessive force against the NYPD declined by nearly half, from one complaint per ten officers to one complaint per nineteen. Shootings by officers also declined 50 percent and was lower under Giuliani than Dinkins. Police shootings were also lower in NYC than in San Diego and Houston, both of which were praised for their "community policing" efforts at that time.

While this is no excuse for police misconduct, the ratio of crimes prevented to misconduct is far too great to oppose policing on the basis that police sometimes do the wrong thing. In the city's 34th Precinct, which includes the majority Hispanic Washington Heights section of Manhattan, murders fell from seventy-six to seven from Dinkins's last year in office to Giuliani's last (a drop of 90 percent).

The Quality of Life Campaign

A large part of Giuliani's campaign was to fix "broken windows" with a crackdown on offenses against the quality of life. If the government couldn't even crack down on minor offenses, what faith could people (and criminals) have that law enforcement would be able to stop violent crimes?

To combat the thousands of so-called squeegee men who roamed the streets, cleaning the windshields of cars stuck in traffic and then demanding payment, sometimes violently, a city law passed in 1996 elevated aggressive panhandling from a violation to a misdemeanor. Giuliani also told police officers that they could simply arrest any panhandlers they came across for jaywalking.

Another quality of life change made an instant impact on the city's aesthetic—cleaning up graffiti. "Graffiti creates an impression of disorder and of lawlessness," Giuliani said. "A city tainted by vandalism invites more vandalism and more serious crime because it sends the message that the city doesn't care and isn't paying attention. In the past, the city has turned a blind eye to this very serious problem that turns public spaces into threatening and menacing areas. However, we've taken the challenge of eliminating graffiti very seriously."[179]

Giuliani formed the Mayor's Anti-Graffiti Task force, nearly eliminating graffiti from 97 percent of parks. In a single year (1996), 6.5 million square feet of graffiti was cleaned from highways and roads. An anti-graffiti squad was formed within the NYPD to enforce laws against graffiti. Those reporting vandals were compensated up to $500.

---

179 "Mayor's Message: Mayor's WINS Address," Archives of Rudolph W. Giuliani, February 23, 1997, http://www.nyc.gov/html/records/rwg/html/97a/me970223.html.

Other crimes targeted included prostitution, jaywalking, public drinking, public urination, and public homelessness.

The Midtown Community Court was created in 1993 in Times Square to swiftly handle those who committed quality of life offenses, such as vandalism, prostitution, and fare evasion.[180]

While police played a major role in reducing crime in New York City, so did simply getting more people on the street who otherwise wouldn't feel safe venturing out. Criminals tend to act at night because there are fewer potential witnesses to report them—but they're more likely to act during the day if the masses are deterred from going out at all.

Years later, Giuliani further strengthened his cleanup by using a precinct-by-precinct computer mapping system to track these kinds of offenses.

While you'd hardly expect it from him today, after police rolled out this program in 1994, Jerry Nadler commented: "Of course a murder or a rape is more important. But in the aggregate, these quality-of-life offenses can destroy a neighborhood and make a park unusable."[181]

Welfare Reform

New York City's welfare reform was yet another Giuliani success story that had the added bonus of reducing crime by putting the unemployed to work.

---

180 George L. Kelling, "How New York Became Safe: The Full Story," *City Journal*, Special Issue 2009, https://www.city-journal.org/html/how-new-york-became-safe-full-story-13197.html.

181 Norimitsu Onishi, "Police Announce Crackdown on Quality-of-Life Offenses," *New York Times*, March 13, 1994, https://www.nytimes.com/1994/03/13/nyregion/police-announce-crackdown-on-quality-of-life-offenses.html.

Mayor John Lindsey began increasing the welfare rolls in 1960s under the justification that there were some people who simply would never be able to make a living for themselves. While that may be true of those with certain mental disabilities or physical conditions, it is not the case for the overwhelming majority of the population, and it's a policy that encourages people who otherwise would be able to better themselves to fall victim to the allure of dependency.

Under Dinkins, NYC's welfare rolls grew by 273,000 people, or one-third. By 1992, the city had 1.1 million on welfare. The increasing trend of dependency continued uninterrupted until Giuliani.

Like the reforms implemented under President Bill Clinton, Giuliani put a strong emphasis on work requirements and sanctioned those who didn't meet requirements. Fewer than 60 percent of cases by the end of 1994 were of individuals subject to mandatory work requirements. By the middle of 1999, nearly 80 percent of those receiving welfare were. The percent sanctioned for noncompliance increased 75 percent from 1996 to 1999.[182]

Knowing how susceptible to fraud the system is, Giuliani first recertified everyone in the city's home-relief program to root out fraud. The city discovered that tens of thousands on the dole were already employed but lied about their work status, lived outside the city, or provided fake Social Security numbers. In under a year, the rolls of the program (which was for able-bodied adults not eligible for federal welfare) were reduced by 20 percent.

And that 20 percent decline was simply from rooting out waste fraud and abuse. Then came the implementation of work

---

182 Demetra Smith Nightingale et al., "Work and Welfare Reform in New York City during the Giuliani Administration: A Study of Program Implementation," Urban Institute Labor and Social Policy Center, July 2002, http://webarchive.urban.org/UploadedPDF/NYC_welfare.pdf.

requirements, forcing recipients to spend thirty-five hours a week cleaning city parks and streets or doing clerical work in municipal offices. Despite the cries from objectors that recipients wouldn't be capable of doing the work, miraculously they were.

By 1999, the welfare rolls had fallen by over six hundred thousand, with over one hundred thousand a year moving from welfare to work. About 75 percent of those placed into jobs remained off welfare a year later, and work rates for NYC's single mothers from 1994–2009 rose from 43 percent to 63 percent, even as the labor force participation rate declined nationally. Child poverty in NYC in 2011 (still recovering from the recession) was ten percentage points below what it was the year before welfare reform began in 1993.

Welfare rolls were reduced nearly 60 percent under Giuliani, from 1.1 million to 462,000. Those declines continued, and only 339,000 were on the dole by the time de Blasio took office in 2014.[183] The drop is even more drastic when you consider the city's population increased by 700,000 during Giuliani's tenure.

In the pre–welfare reform era (1972–1993) one in ten welfare recipients in the entire country lived in New York City. That ratio fell to one in twenty-five by 2014. This drop amounted to the largest drop in welfare dependency in the U.S. over a twenty-year period.

Enter: Bill de Blasio

Fast forward to now and we have current Mayor Bill de Blasio pushing the opposite agenda. As we're informed by de Blasio's

---

183 "Dependency vs. Opportunity in New York City," Manhattan Institute, 2014, https://media4.manhattan-institute.org/sites/cj/files/old/assets/images/25_2-fs2.pdf.

own biography page: "He began his career in public service in 1989 as part of David N. Dinkins' successful and historic mayoral campaign and worked in the Dinkins Administration."[184]

Opposing the city's "stop-and-frisk" policy began a central part of his campaign." He released a report critical of the practice in 2012 and months later took part in a silent march against it. In a thirty-second 2013 campaign ad entitled "Dignity," de Blasio fully denounced the practice, invoking his then fifteen-year-old biracial son, Dante, and an alleged "conversation about the police" he and his wife, Chirlane, had with him. "Chirlane and I have talked to Dante many times about the fact that some day you will be stopped."[185]

Dante de Blasio had never been stopped by police, nor did any evidence suggest such a stop was inevitable, but the ad allowed de Blasio to tout himself as a "father who, although white, understood what it is like to raise young people of color who must navigate racist, state-sanctioned violence."

So right off the bat, the NYPD was told by its new mayor-to-be that he doesn't even trust the officers around his kids and that he believes its force (which is majority-minority) is racist.

De Blasio's ad stated that he was "the only candidate to end a stop-and-frisk era that targets minorities," and indeed, de Blasio was more explicit than primary opponents Thompson or Quinn in his condemnation of the practice. The de Blasio campaign platform supported two City Council bills, one banning racial profiling (which is already illegal) and the other creating an

---

184 "Bill de Blasio: 109th Mayor of New York City," Official Website of the City of New York, https://www1.nyc.gov/office-of-the-mayor/bio.page.

185 Michael Barbaro, "The Ad Campaign: De Blasio Speaks against Stop-and-Frisk Tactics," *New York Times*, August 19, 2013, https://cityroom.blogs.nytimes.com/2013/08/19/the-ad-campaign-de-blasio-speaks-against-stop-and-frisk/.

inspector general in the police department. De Blasio also vowed to replace Raymond Kelly as commissioner.

District Judge Shira Scheindlin would do most of his work for him and found the NYPD's use of stop-and-frisk unconstitutional a month before the mayoral primary. Scheindlin was later removed from the court for "failing to appear impartial by making public statements about the case" and for granting media interviews where she addressed critics,[186] and the ruling was appealed, but de Blasio withdrew the appeal as mayor.[187]

Mayor Michael Bloomberg asserted that Judge Scheindlin did not reflect an "understanding of how policing works," and that "any changes in tactics would not come overnight" and appealed the ruling. Bloomberg called de Blasio's use of his family in the campaign "racist" and accused him of advocating "class warfare," which some believe resulted in an unintentional de Blasio boost.

Stops collapsed thereafter from a peak of over 685,000 in 2011 to only 11,629 by 2017.[188]

Bill Bratton, who ran the NYPD under Giuliani from 1994–1996, also served a term as de Blasio's police commissioner from 2014–2016. He made his stance on stop-and-frisk clear: you can't police without it. "Stop, question and frisk is a basic tool

---

186 Joseph Ax, "Court Halts NYC Stop-and-Frisk Ruling, Removes Judge," Reuters, October 31, 2013, https://www.reuters.com/article/us-usa-newyork-stopandfrisk-ruling/court-halts-nyc-stop-and-frisk-ruling-removes-judge-idUSBRE99U1A120131031.

187 "NYC Mayor Bill de Blasio Settles in Stop-and-Frisk Case," NPR, January 31, 2014, https://www.npr.org/transcripts/269530085?storyId=269530085?storyId=269530085.

188 Michelle Shames and Simon McCormack, "Stop and Frisks Plummeted under New York Mayor Bill de Blasio, but Racial Disparities Haven't Budged," ACLU, March 14, 2019, https://www.aclu.org/blog/criminal-law-reform/reforming-police/stop-and-frisks-plummeted-under-new-york-mayor-bill-de.

of policing—not only American policing, around the world. But in United States, it's defined by the *Terry vs. Ohio* Supreme Court decision back in the 1960s, which articulated when police can stop and for what purpose. So every police department in America every day does it," he said in a radio interview.

"The way it was practiced here for the last number of years is that it was overused. And it's the overuse that then created the negative reaction to the basic policy itself. And the confusion about whether you can police with or without it. You cannot police without it, I'm sorry. It's—if you did not have it, then you'd have anarchy, being quite frank with you."[189] Bratton agreed with de Blasio that there were too many stops—but certainly not too many to justify the 98 percent decline from the 2011 peak.

During a 2014 press conference where he announced his intent to drop the appeal of Scheindlin's ruling, de Blasio stated, "We're here today to turn the page on one of the most divisive problems in our city. We believe in ending the overuse of stop-and-frisk that has unfairly targeted young African-American and Latino men."

De Blasio had chosen the Brownsville Recreation Center as the venue for the press conference, symbolic because the center is located in a neighborhood of Brooklyn where the stop-and-frisk tactics had been widely applied.

Standing next to him were the directors of the civil rights legal groups that had pursued the two lawsuits covered by the agreement, and some of the NYPD's vociferous critics.

---

189 "Bill Bratton: You Can't Police without Stop-and-Frisk," WBUR, February 25, 2014, https://www.wbur.org/hereandnow/2014/02/25/bill-bratton-nypd.

That stop-and-frisk was "racist" was the entirety of the case against the practice. As is common for the left, de Blasio relied on statistical disparities to make that accusation without bothering to uncover the actual cause of those disparities. The de Blasio case is as follows: At the height of stop-and-frisk in New York City in 2011, police made 685,724 stops. Blacks accounted for 52.9 percent of those stopped, Latinos 33.7 percent, whites 9.3 percent, and Asians and American Indians 4 percent.[190] For context, NYC is 24.3 percent African American and 29.1 percent Hispanic or Latino.[191]

De Blasio believes that stop-and-frisk should be proportional to representation in the overall population (for example, if race "X" is 10 percent of the population, they should account for 10 percent of the stops).

The problem with de Blasio's philosophy is that unless we live in a world where every demographic commits crime at exactly the same rate, there will always be a statistical disparity to point to as proof of racism, and the source of this disparity is always blamed on law enforcement, not the perpetrators themselves. The only actual way to even out the statistics would be to arrest fewer criminals from demographics committing a disproportionate share of crimes, which would in turn encourage more crime. Most of the victims would be individuals from the same communities as the perpetrators.

---

190 "Stop-and-Frisk 2011," New York Civil Liberties Union, May 9, 2012, https://www.nyclu.org/sites/default/files/publications/NYCLU_2011_Stop-and-Frisk_Report.pdf

191 "QuickFacts: New York City, New York," U.S. Census Bureau, https://www.census.gov/quickfacts/fact/table/newyorkcitynewyork/RHI225219#RHI225219.

What stop-and-frisk arrests should be measured against isn't a demographic representation in the overall population, but their representation as perpetrators of crimes. For example, NYC's murder suspects were 35 percent Hispanic and 56.3 percent black in 2011. For rape, the figures were 48.8 percent black and 34.5 percent Hispanic. For robbery, the figures were 70.6 percent black and 24 percent Hispanic. In this context, stop-and-frisk stops are underrepresenting non-whites.[192]

Even while stops have cratered, six years following the end of stop-and-frisk practices, blacks still account for 48 percent of arrests in NYC.[193] The racial breakdown on arrestees remains consistent, the data shows. Meanwhile, crime is on the rise once again, with all data indicating that the end of stop-and-frisk has not reduced any disparity in arrests and, arguably, criminality rate, but only in the number of arrests that would have deterred violent crimes.

Michael Bloomberg defended the program against those bogus allegations of racism in 2013, pointing out the politically incorrect truth that whites are actually overrepresented in stop-and-frisk encounters relative to the number of crimes they tend to commit. "I think we disproportionately stop whites too much and minorities too little," he said in an interview on WOR Radio. It's an accurate commentary on the statistics, though of course

---

192 "Crime and Enforcement Activity in New York City: Jan. 1–December 31, 2011," NYPD, https://www1.nyc.gov/assets/nypd/downloads/pdf/analysis_and_planning/yearend2011enforcementreport.pdf.

193 Bill Hutchinson, "Blacks Account for Nearly Half of All NYC Arrests 6 Years After End of Stop-and-Frisk: NYPD Data," ABC News, June 30, 2020, https://abcnews.go.com/US/blacks-account-half-nyc-arrests-years-end-stop/story?id=71412485.

without context it's a comment that sounds godawful for a presidential candidate when played back.

He echoed the same point in a 2015 interview: "You are arresting kids for marijuana that are all minorities. Yes, that's true. Why? Because we put all the cops in the minority neighborhoods. Yes, that's true. Why do we do it? Because that's where all the crime is. And the way you get the guns out of the kids' hands is to throw them up against the walls and frisk them."[194] It's indeed the case that if you have more police in an area due to violent crime, police are bound to also enforce laws on lesser crimes (in this case, marijuana possession). Marijuana has since been decriminalized in New York in 2019.

Bloomberg would later have to pretend to have been wrong during his brief stint incinerating a billion dollars while running for president.

Bill de Blasio's Tumultuous Relationship with Police

In the middle of 2019, a Twitter video went viral, showing NYPD officers in Harlem being drenched with buckets of water by a number of young men while making an arrest. Onlookers stood by and laughed. At the end of the video, the officers walked away drenched as some continued flinging water at them.

The incident was symptomatic of the extent to which de Blasio had castrated the police, and it was something that had happened gradually since he took office.

---

194 Courtney Gross, "Bloomberg Defends Stop-and-Frisk Use on Minority Communities in Resurfaced 2015 Audio," NY1, February 11, 2020, https://www.ny1.com/nyc/all-boroughs/politics/2020/02/12/mike-bloomberg-stop-and-frisk-audio-resurfaces-accused-of-racism.

A police source blamed de Blasio's "hands-off approach to these guys." The source continued, "Who does that in their right frame of mind? People who believe there's no consequences. There's total anarchy out here. This is very sad."[195]

The head of the NYPD's Police Benevolent Association said the attacks were "the end result of the torrent of bad policies and anti-police rhetoric that has been streaming out of City Hall and Albany for years now. We are approaching the point of no return. Disorder controls the streets, and our elected leaders refuse to allow us to take them back."

He continued, "As police officers, we need to draw a line. In situations like this, we need to take action to protect ourselves and the public. The politicians may not care about the dangerous levels of chaos in our neighborhoods, but police officers and decent New Yorkers should not be forced to suffer."

De Blasio's relationship with the police is a tumultuous one, continuously escalating since he took office.[196]

- April 22, 2014: De Blasio resists calls for one thousand more cops.
- July 17, 2014: Eric Garner is killed by police on Staten Island.

---

195 Tina Moore, Larry Celona, Craig McCarthy, and Bruce Golding, "NYPD Cops Get Drenched by Buckets of Water," *New York Post*, July 22, 2019, https://nypost.com/2019/07/22/total-anarchy-nypd-cops-get-drenched-by-buckets-of-water/.

196 This article served as a template for the timeline through 2017. Jarrett Murphy, "Timeline: The Saga of Bill de Blasio and the NYPD," *City Limits*, October 16, 2017, https://citylimits.org/2017/10/16/timeline-the-saga-of-bill-de-blasio-and-the-nypd/.

- July 31, 2014: De Blasio sits next to Rev. Al Sharpton at a discussion at City Hall in the wake of the Garner killing in a move widely criticized.
- August 27, 2014: The head of the sergeants' union takes out a full-page ad discouraging the DNC from selecting New York for its next convention, claiming that crime is resurgent.
- November 14, 2014: De Blasio signs bills that restrict cooperation between the police and jail system with federal immigration enforcement.
- December 2, 2014: A grand jury decides not to indict the officer who put his arm around Eric Garner's neck. De Blasio reacts to the news by talking about discussing with his son the possibility of a dangerous encounter with the police.
- December 13, 2014: A massive, "mostly peaceful" march takes place to protest police violence after the Garner non-indictment. Video later emerges of protesters chanting "What do we want? Dead cops." Another group of protestors fights with officers on the Brooklyn Bridge.
- December 20, 2014: Officers Rafael Ramos and Wenjian Liu are killed in Brooklyn. Cops gathered at the hospital turn their backs on de Blasio as he walks down the halls. Police Benevolent Association (then the Patrolmen's Benevolent Association) president Pat Lynch says "there is blood on many hands," referring specifically to de Blasio.
- December 27, 2014: Officers turn their backs on de Blasio at Ramos's funeral.
- December 29, 2014: De Blasio booed at NYPD graduation.

- January 7, 2015: Reports surface of an NYPD work slow-down, reportedly out of anger toward the mayor.
- May 2015: The NYPD launches Neighborhood Coordination Officers in four precincts, the start of a new take on community policing.
- June 2, 2015: *New York Post*: "Just how many New Yorkers must die before Mayor de Blasio lets cops bring back stop-and-frisk?"
- June 22, 2015: Under pressure by Council leadership and seeing an uptick in crime, de Blasio agrees to add 1,300 cops to budget.
- August 6, 2015: De Blasio unveils NYC Safe, a mental-health initiative with a focus on policing.
- September 22, 2015: *New York Post*: "Mayor de Blasio wants New Yorkers to think they needn't worry about crime spiking. The facts suggest otherwise."
- October 20, 2015: Officer Randolph Holder is killed in a Harlem shootout.
- October 23, 2015: After Holder's death, de Blasio calls for public safety considerations in deciding whether and at what amount to set bail.
- November 5, 2015: In a move widely regarded as intended to embarrass de Blasio, Governor Cuomo boosts the New York State Police presence in New York City.
- January 25, 2016: The mayor agrees to a City Council plan to decriminalize certain low-level offenses, allowing cops to issue tickets instead of arrests or criminal summonses. The offenses for which criminal penalties are eliminated include drinking alcohol in public, spitting, urinating, and littering on the street or in building lobbies.

- April 8, 2016: The mayor announces a bail alternative program that amounts to an expansion of the city's supervised release program.
- September 7, 2016: The NYPD releases research promoting the efficacy of broken-windows policing.
- October 23, 2016: Police Benevolent Association President Pat Lynch declares, "This is the most difficult time to be a police officer in my 32 years on the job. We're getting screwed at every turn. We're not getting support from City Hall."[197]
- March 31, 2017: De Blasio announces support for a ten-year timetable for closing Rikers Island.
- May 12, 2017: The mayor unveils a $90 million program to reduce low-level arrests for people with behavioral health needs.
- May 22, 2017: NYPD commissioner James O'Neill says he won't march in the Puerto Rican Day parade honoring militant Oscar Lopez Rivera, which de Blasio takes part in.
- July 5, 2017: Officer Miosotis Familia is killed as she sits in an NYPD vehicle on a Bronx street. De Blasio leaves the city later that week for a speech in Germany.
- July 11, 2017: Hundreds of NYPD officers turn their backs on de Blasio at the funeral for Officer Familia.
- July 12, 2017: The Mayor's Office attempts to deny that NYPD officers turned their backs on de Blasio.

---

197 Emily Saul, "De Blasio 'Neutered' New Commissioner: Police Union Boss," *New York Post*, October 23, 2016, https://nypost.com/2016/10/23/de-blasio-neutered-new-commissioner-police-union-boss/.

- December 12, 2017: De Blasio backs the Right to Know Act, a package of police reform bills.
- January 9, 2018: The Police Benevolent Association sues de Blasio and the NYPD commissioner for releasing police bodycam footage, citing the "arbitrary and inconsistent" nature of the release that appears motivated by political considerations.[198]
- January 30, 2018: De Blasio announces that all officers will wear body cameras by the end of 2018, a year earlier than expected.[199]
- March 11, 2018: All NYPD cops assigned to NYC public schools are moved out in the wake of the Parkland school shooting.
- June 16, 2018: De Blasio announces that NYPD won't arrest people for smoking marijuana in public anymore. The policy takes effect on September 1.
- July 3, 2018: De Blasio moves to revise governing document for the city's 5,300+ school safety agents who work in public schools.
- July 5, 2018: De Blasio uses a $3 million NYPD counter-terrorism plane to fly home from vacation.

198 Gloria Pazmino, "Police Union Sues de Blasio Administration, NYPD over Release of Body Cam Footage," Politico, January 9, 2018, https://www.politico.com/states/new-york/albany/story/2018/01/09/police-union-sues-de-blasio-administration-over-release-of-body-worn-camera-footage-177414.
199 "De Blasio Administration, NYPD Announce All Officers on Patrol to Wear Body Cameras by End of 2018, One Year Earlier Than Expected," Official Website of the City of New York, January 30, 2018, https://www1.nyc.gov/office-of-the-mayor/news/071-18/de-blasio-administration-nypd-all-officers-patrol-wear-body-cameras-end-2018-#/0.

- July 19, 2018: The federal judge overseeing stop-and-frisk related cases orders the NYPD to record lower-level encounters that don't rise to a full police stop.[200]
- August 12, 2018: De Blasio is heckled and booed at NYPD graduation.
- August 22, 2018: Police Benevolent Association president charges that "de Blasio and company have turned the streets against the NYPD."
- April 9, 2019: De Blasio says he's concerned about cops who drive recklessly and vows action.
- May 16, 2019: De Blasio announces run for president, generating excitement from tens of supporters.
- June 23, 2019: De Blasio issues new guidelines that prohibit NYPD officers from arresting students or issuing summonses for offenses including graffiti and marijuana possession.
- June 24, 2019: NYC PBA travels to Miami for the Democratic debate to remind de Blasio how much they dislike him. De Blasio says on the debate stage regarding police, "For the last 21 years I've been raising a black son in America, and I have had to have very, very serious talks with my son Dante about how to protect himself on the streets of our city and all over this country, including how to deal with the fact that he has to take special caution because there's been too many tragedies between our young men and our police, too."

---

200 Brendan Cheney, "Politico: Judge Orders NYPD to Enact Pilot Program on Low-Level Stops," The Bronx Defenders, July 19, 2018, https://www.bronxdefenders.org/politico-judge-orders-nypd-to-enact-pilot-program-on-low-level-stops/.

- June 27, 2019: After one of the Democratic presidential debates, the NYC PBA releases the statement: "Mayor de Blasio has apparently learned nothing over the past six years about the extremely damaging impact of anti-police rhetoric on both cops and the communities we serve."[201]
- July 1, 2019: De Blasio defends an op-ed written by his son, in which he says that he's afraid to interact with the police.
- July 2, 2019: NYPD unions blast de Blasio for being friendly with them to their faces while publicly talking about his fears of his black son being stopped by police.[202]
- July 25, 2019: In the past week, at least four videos come to light showing officers being doused with water on separate occasions while onlookers laugh. The officers don't engage in any of these cases. Giuliani calls de Blasio a "disgrace."
- August 4, 2019: *New York Daily News* reports that de Blasio ordered an NYPD Executive Protection Unit to help move his daughter out of her Brooklyn apartment.
- August 14, 2019: De Blasio says he's reformed policing and improved police community relations.

---

201 Zack Budryk, "New York Police Union Blasts de Blasio's Comments on Cops in Debate," The Hill, June 27, 2019, https://thehill.com/homenews/campaign/450644-new-york-police-union-blasts-de-blasios-comments-on-cops-in-debate.

202 "NYPD Unions Not Happy with de Blasio's Two-Faced Attitude towards Police in America," CBS New York, July 2, 2019, https://newyork.cbslocal.com/2019/07/02/mayor-bill-de-blasio-campaign-20209-nypd-dante-de-blasio/.

- August 28, 2019: NYPD union unanimously approves a resolution of "no confidence" against de Blasio and Commissioner James O'Neill, and again calls on Governor Cuomo to remove de Blasio from office.
- September 2019: De Blasio drops out of presidential race.
- October 28, 2019: *New York Daily News* reports that de Blasio used his NYPD security detail to move his kid to college.

And from the start of the new decade, de Blasio put the pedal to the floor in implementing godawful policies (in one case with an assist from Cuomo).

The Bail Reform Disaster

New York's bail reform law is one passed by Governor Cuomo, championed by de Blasio, and was immediately such a catastrophic failure that even he couldn't pretend otherwise.

A sane person would probably conclude that the abolition of bail would make criminals more likely to commit crimes. And not only would it make them more likely to commit crimes, it would increase the number of those immediately reoffending.

Unfortunately, sane individuals appear rare in New York's government.

Like any other progressive proposal, there's how we're told it will work in theory, and then there's reality. In this case, it worked in neither. We were told that only those who committed nonviolent crimes would be allowed to skip bail. Before it took effect, de Blasio said, "In a world where we want speedier trials and we want the justice system to work, if small incentives are part of what actually makes it work, then that's a smart policy."[203] Cuomo was equally optimistic, telling critics that these reforms are "long overdue."[204]

In total, New York's new bail reform eliminated cash bail for 90 percent of arrests, enabling defendants to await trial at home. Crimes that no longer required bail included suspects accused of second-degree manslaughter, aggravated vehicular assault, third-degree assault, criminally negligent homicide, and aggravated vehicular homicide, among nearly a hundred other crimes.

The law took effect on New Year's Day 2020, and the consequences were immediately made clear.

One man alleged to be a subway thief boasted after being released following his 139th career arrest, "I'm famous! I take $200, $300 a day of your money, cracker! You can't stop me! It's a great thing. It's a beautiful thing. They punk'ed people out for bullsh– crimes."[205] "Bail reform—it's lit!" he added. He was jailed weeks later—after his 142nd arrest.[206]

---

203 "Bail Reform: Mayor de Blasio Defends Giving Freed Prison Inmates Gifts for Appearing in Court as 'a Smart Policy,'" CBS New York, November 6, 2019, https://newyork.cbslocal.com/2019/11/06/de-blasio-inmates-gifts-court/.

204 Barry N. Covert, "Gov. Andrew Cuomo Addresses Concerns over New York State Bail Reform," Lipsitz Green Scime Cambria, December 5, 2019, https://www.lipsitzgreen.com/blog/2019/12/05/gov-andrew-cuomo-addresses-concerns-over-new-york-state-bail-reform/.

205 Danielle Wallace, "NYC Subway Thief Thanks Democrats after His 139th Arrest, Release: 'Bail Reform. It's Lit!'" Fox News, February 16, 2020, https://www.foxnews.com/us/new-york-bail-reform-law-nyc-subway-thief-thanks-democrats-139th-arrest.

206 Rebecca Rosenberg, Olivia Bensimon, Elizabeth Rosner, and Laura Italiano, "Serial Manhattan Subway Scammer Jailed after 142nd Arrest," *New York Post*, February 27, 2020, https://nypost.com/2020/02/27/serial-manhattan-subway-scammer-jailed-after-142nd-arrest/.

It wasn't just petty thieves benefitting from bail reform either. In October 2018, thirty-five-year-old Army veteran Hason Correa was fatally stabbed nine times in front of his dad in the lobby of a West 152nd Street apartment building. Correa's father was also stabbed and survived. Four people were accused in connection with the crime: Mary Saunders (accused of grabbing and holding Correa as he attempted to flee), two men responsible for the physical stabbing (who are brothers of Saunders), and a fourth person who with Saunders chased Correa when he tried to flee. Correa's mother said she believes the attackers were Bloods members retaliating over a scuffle earlier in the night that her son wasn't part of.

Saunders initially faced charges of second-degree murder and $700,000 bail after her arrest, which she couldn't post. Following the new bail law, that bail was reduced to $12,000, and she posted bail right after reform took effect.

Correa's mother appeared on Pix 11's *Mary Murphy Files* to discuss the miscarriage of justice. As she pointed out, both murder and first-degree gang assault are supposed to be exempt from NY's anti-bail law. Under the new bail laws, the judge could only impose a bail on Saunders "that she could afford." The judge told Correa's mother that her "hands were tied" and she wanted Saunders to stay in jail but couldn't keep her locked up.[207]

Just three months into bail reform, the NYPD cited it as a significant reason behind the immediate spike in crime. In just the first two months of the year, the NYPD released statistics showing that nearly five hundred suspects who would've

---

207 Matt Palumbo, "NY's Anti-Bail Reforms Help Free Alleged Murderer of Army Vet," *Dan Bongino Show*, January 7, 2020, https://bongino.com/nys-anti-bail-reforms-help-free-alleged-murderer-of-army-vet/.

otherwise been in jail awaiting trial committed an additional 846 crimes they wouldn't have otherwise had the opportunity to commit. Nearly three hundred of those crimes included murder, rape, robbery, felony assault, burglary, grand larceny, and grand larceny auto.[208]

The number of crimes going to trial also fell. Prosecutors in NYC declined to prosecute 11 percent of all non-bail-eligible felony arrests in January and February, or 803 crimes. The year prior they declined to prosecute 527, or 6.7 percent of all non-bail felony arrests.

There were 16,343 "major crimes" reported in the first two months of 2020 compared to 13,648 the year prior. Those released on bail reform made up nearly 2 percent of the entire crimes in the city for the year and caused 10 percent of the spike.

It was reported that on April 3 Cuomo signed into law a state budget that reversed key reforms to the bail system, but that doesn't seem to have materialized.[209] Even as rioters sought to loot and burn the city to the ground, bail reform protected the perpetrators. Of over 650 arrests made in a single night of protests on June 1, nearly every single one was released without bail. NYC police chief Terence Monahan told the *New York Post* that "when it comes to a burglary [at] a commercial store, which is looting, they're back out... Because of bail reform, you're back out on the street the next day. You cannot be held on any sort

---

208 John Binder, "Over 400 NYC Looters to Be Freed from Jail Thanks to 'Bail Reform' Policy," Breitbart, June 2, 2020, https://www.breitbart.com/ politics/2020/06/02/over-400-nyc-looters-to-be-freed-from-jail-thanks-to-bail-reform-policy/.

209 Alexander Lekhtman, "NY Gov. Cuomo Signs Away Bail Reforms Despite COVID-19 Decarceration Calls," *Filter*, April 9, 2020, https://filtermag. org/ny-governor-cuomo-bail-reforms/.

of bail. I spoke to [Manhattan district attorney] Cy Vance about that, he told me there's nothing he can do."[210]

COVID Chaos

The pandemic revealed that New York's leaders did care about law and order after all, so long as the force of the law was brought down on small business owners and those otherwise looking to go on with their lives, or people who only keep five feet and eleven inches apart.

While the state and city crushed businesses that didn't fully comply with pandemic regulations with fines, and fined citizens who didn't social distance properly or wear a mask, no such rules applied to the "mostly peaceful protesters" who took to the streets, nor those who turned to violence.

No such disdain that de Blasio gave toward Jews attending funerals was directed at criminals looting his city and burning it to the ground. Ordinary people wanting haircuts were branded selfish, while those chanting for dead cops were excused as "mostly peaceful" protesters.

And that's just the tip of the iceberg when it comes to horrible decisions made during the pandemic.

NYC (and many other cities with liberal leaders) used this as an opportunity to release prisoners under the logic that they would be less likely to catch the virus in the outside world than in prison. Over 1,500 inmates in NYC were granted early release. At

---

210 Zachary Evans, "Police Chief: Arrested Looters in NYC Are Immediately Released Because of Bail-Reform Law," *National Review*, June 2, 2020. https://www.nationalreview.com/news/george-floyd-protests-arrested-looters-in-new-york-city-are-immediately-released-due-to-bail-reform-law/.

least 250 of them were quickly rearrested for new crimes (and in some cases, then cut loose again).[211]

In response to the entirely predictable consequences of his actions, de Blasio said that it was "unconscionable" that seasoned criminals would commit crimes after being handed a "get out of jail free" card.[212]

Plainclothes Unit Disbanded

On June 15, Commissioner Dermot Shea made a surprise announcement: that the city would be disbanding its plainclothes anti-crime unit. Shea justified the decision by calling the force part of an "outdated model of policing," and said that the former plainclothes unit would be reassigned to the detective bureau and the NYPD's neighborhood policing initiative.

De Blasio said he supported Commissioner Shea's decision to disband the plainclothes anti-crime unit, explaining "the NYPD can replace the Anti-crime Unit with technology, precision policing" and "not have the negative of some of the concerns that have been raised by the community."[213]

Upon learning of the announcement, retired NYPD Sergeant Joseph Giacalone warned that a violent summer was around the

---

211 Melissa Russo, "NYPD Brass: We're Arresting Too Many Prisoners on Early COVID Release," NBC New York, June 12, 2020, https://www.nbcnewyork.com/news/local/crime-and-courts/released-from-rikers-in-covid-measure-man-arrested-4-times-in-3-months/2460035/.

212 Julia Marsh and Jorge Fitz-Gibbon, "Inmates Committing Crimes After Coronavirus Release 'Unconscionable': de Blasio." *New York Post*, April 20, 2020, https://nypost.com/2020/04/20/unconscionable-for-released-inmates-to-commit-crimes-de-blasio/.

213 Bill Hutchinson, "Blacks Account for Nearly Half of All NYC Arrests 6 Years After End of Stop-and-Frisk: NYPD Data," ABC News, June 30, 2020, https://abcnews.go.com/US/blacks-account-half-nyc-arrests-years-end-stop/story?id=71412485.

corner. "You couple this with no bail for anyone who even gets arrested for these illegal firearms. You have a massive release of prisoners earlier," said Giacalone. "This is kind of a cocktail of waiting for disaster to happen."[214]

Those predictions materialized quickly.

According to an NYPD press release, "the number of people murdered citywide increased to 39 v. 30, (+30%) for the month [of June], while the number of burglaries increased to 1,783 v. 817 (+118%) and the number of auto thefts increased to 696 v. 462 (+51%) citywide."[215]

In the press release for the June statistics, the NYPD notes that it is "enduring a round of deep budget cuts that have led to a class of 1,163 recruits being canceled. The department has also seen an increase in retirements. The NYPD's facilitation of peaceful protest continues to utilize department resources. While the NYPD uses a lighter touch in regard to enforcement, offenders no longer eligible for bail are being rearrested: they have been rearrested for approximately 750 additional major felonies through June 26, compared with the population of those released in the same period a year ago."

By August, the city had more shootings than the entire year of 2019, with 777 shootings.[216] By the end of the month, they

---

214 Rocco Vertuccio, "Disbanding NYPD Plainclothes Anti-Crime Unit Gets Mixed Reaction," Spectrum News NY 1, June 17, 2020, https://www.ny1.com/nyc/all-boroughs/news/2020/06/17/disbanding-nypd-plainclothes-anti-crime-unit-gets-mixed-reaction.

215 "NYPD Announces Citywide Crime Statistics for June 2020," NYPD, July 6, 2020, https://www1.nyc.gov/site/nypd/news/pr0706/nypd-citywide-crime-statistics-june-2020.

216 Todd Maisel, "NYC Shootings: Six More Wounded as NYC Surpasses Shooting Total from 2019," AMNY, August 2, 2020, https://www.amny.com/news/nyc-shootings-six-more-wounded-as-nyc-surpasses-shooting-total-from-2019/.

surpassed 1,000 shootings.[217] Shootings in 2020 are on track to surpass 2018 and 2019 combined,[218] and only 20 percent of shootings are now ending in arrests.[219]

Meanwhile, de Blasio employed new logic to explain away what was happening: guns don't kill people, coronavirus does. "I want to talk about what happened this weekend. Many were out there celebrating, but we saw too much violence, and we have a lot of work to do to address it," de Blasio said, while adding that "there is not one cause for something like this. This is directly related to coronavirus. This is a very serious situation…. As we're getting into warmer and warmer weather, we're feeling the effects of people being cooped up for months, the economy hasn't restarted—we have a real problem here."[220] De Blasio later said the coronavirus vaccine will end NYC's shooting epidemic.[221]

217 Craig McCarthy and Larry Celona, "NYC Passes Grim Gun-Violence Milestone as Shootings Top 1,000 for the Year," *New York Post*, August 31, 2020, https://nypost.com/2020/08/31/nyc-passes-grim-milestone-with-over-1000-shootings-in-2020/.

218 AWR Hawkins, "Shootings in de Blasio's NYC on Track to Surpass 2018, 2019 Combined," Breitbart, August 10, 2020, https://www.breitbart.com/politics/2020/08/10/shootings-in-de-blasios-nyc-on-track-to-surpass-2018-2019-combined/.

219 Craig McCarthy and Aaron Feis, "NYPD Data: Only About 20 Percent of NYC Shootings Ended in Arrests This Year," *New York Post*, September 6, 2020, https://nypost.com/2020/09/06/nypd-shooting-arrest-rate-barely-tops-20-percent-as-gunplay-surges/.

220 Brooke Singman, "De Blasio Blames NYC Weekend Violence on Coronavirus, Vows to 'Double Down' to Keep City Safe," Fox News, July 6, 2020, https://www.foxnews.com/politics/de-blasio-blames-nyc-weekend-violence-on-coronavirus-vows-to-double-down-to-keep-city-safe.

221 Craig McCarthy and Julia Marsh, "De Blasio Claims COVID-19 Vaccine Will Cure NYC Shooting Epidemic," *New York Post*, September 2, 2020, https://nypost.com/2020/09/02/de-blasio-claims-covid-19-vaccine-will-cure-nyc-shooting-epidemic/.

Alexandria Ocasio-Cortez echoed the same rhetoric, comically declaring that people are simply shoplifting to feed their children. "Maybe this has to do with the fact that people aren't paying their rent and are scared to pay their rent and so they go out, and they need to feed their child and they don't have money." Ocasio-Cortez continued, "So they feel like they either need to shoplift some bread or go hungry."[222] Of course, shoplifting bread isn't the kind of crime that usually results in murder.

This theory is easily refutable on the basis that the exact sort of "crimes of necessity" that Ocasio-Cortez describes are not the types of crimes on the increase. Reports of petit larceny by shoplifting and grand larceny by shoplifting were actually down compared to the previous year. Burglaries were up, but no home invader since Santa Claus has ever made off with food.

To address the spike in crime, de Blasio proposed an increase in foot patrols just weeks after disbanding the plainclothes unit. In effect, all that would change within the course of a few short months would be what clothes those patrolling the streets were wearing. De Blasio implementing some part of his progressive vision before immediately being mugged by reality is a common theme of his administration. It's too bad he never seems to learn from it.

Among the other policies de Blasio proposed included acts of political theater, such as a proposed gun buyback. The policy of paying law-abiding gun owners is one that practically guarantees only law-abiding gun owners turn in their guns, making it a gigantic waste of money if the goal is to reduce crime.

---

222 Yael Halon, "AOC Suggests NYC Crime Surge Due to Unemployment, Residents Who Need to 'Shoplift Some Bread,'" Fox News, July 12, 2020, https://www.foxnews.com/politics/alexandria-ocasio-cortez-nyc-crime-shoplifting.

A study published in the *International Review of Law and Economics* has shown that gun buyback programs in the U.S. can, on net balance, actually increase the supply of firearms in circulation.[223] The study differentiates between two types of buybacks: buybacks that occur in an area once and perpetual buybacks. Single buybacks only temporarily reduce the stock of guns, as many of those who turn in their guns just buy more down the road. As for perpetual buybacks, gun owners can see them as a type of insurance against buyer's remorse, making someone more likely to purchase a firearm. Firearms aren't cheap, so wouldn't it be great to know that if you don't like yours, you can just sell it at a gun buyback and use the money toward another?

Defund the Police

Almost immediately after the death of George Floyd, progressive leaders nationwide collectively hopped on the "defund the police" bandwagon, pushing the narrative that police are racist against blacks. As they did this, polling showed that 81 percent of blacks, the group these progressives claim to speak on behalf of, opposed any reduction to their local police presence.[224]

De Blasio slashed $1 billion from the NYPD's budget, which was $6 billion in 2020. Nearly half were direct cuts, and the other half reallocated funds to have other agencies carry out duties previously done by the police. The idea that cops can be replaced with social workers is among the latest trendy ideas on

---

223 Wallace P. Mullin, "Will Gun Buyback Programs Increase the Quantity of Guns?" *International Review of Law and Economics* 21.1 (March 2001): 87–102, https://www.sciencedirect.com/science/article/abs/pii/S0144818800000521.

224 Lydia Saad, "Black Americans Want Police to Retain Local Presence," Gallup, August 5, 2020, https://news.gallup.com/poll/316571/black-americans-police-retain-local-presence.aspx.

the left with no supporting evidence whatsoever. Of those direct cuts, $300 million are to police overtime. Just in response to the George Floyd riots alone, the NYPD racked up $115 million in overtime costs.

A police class with 1,163 rookies was cut—right as the force saw a wave of early retirements due to poor morale.[225] In the month and a half since the Floyd protests began, 306 officers retired, 40 resigned, and 503 filed for retirement—a 411 percent increase over the same time period last year.[226] Chris Monahan, president of the Captains Endowment Association, left no doubt as to why that was. "Of course cops are retiring at a higher rate. We've been abandoned by the NYPD and elected officials." The Police Benevolent Association echoed similar sentiments: "How are we supposed to do our job in this environment?"

There are two schools of thought on what "defund the police" actually means. Some leftists chanting the phrase claim they merely want to outsource certain police functions to social workers and use funds previously allocated to law enforcement to do so. If that's the case, they ought to find a better slogan. Others, like Ocasio-Cortez, say the quiet part out loud when it comes to what the far-left truly wants: "Defunding the police means defunding the

---

225 Richard Khavkine, "Police Class with 1,163 Rookies among Budget Cuts for NYPD," *The Chief*, July 1, 2020, updated July 10, 2020, https://thechief leader.com/news/news_of_the_week/police-class-with-1-163-rookies-among-budget-cuts-for-nypd/article_b847e326-bbd5-11ea-b783-8b323d54232e.html.

226 Jason Lemon, "NYC Police Retirements Surged 411 Percent Since George Floyd Protests—Here's Why," *Newsweek*, July 14, 2020, https://www.newsweek.com/nyc-police-retirements-surged-411-percent-since-george-floyd-protestsheres-why-1517751.

police. It does not mean budget tricks or funny math…. This is not a victory. The fight to defund policing continues."[227]

Not long after all this, the NYPD union would make its first ever endorsement for a presidential candidate, endorsing President Trump.

The Return of Broken Windows

Broken windows have returned to New York City—and not just because of the rioters de Blasio has enabled.

Graffiti is once again on the rise in the city, popping up on storefronts, buildings, construction barricades—and more. The city's 311 service (which handles requests for government and non-emergency services) is no longer taking graffiti complaints, and the Graffiti-Free NYC removal program has been suspended.

Subway graffiti began exploding in 2019—costing $619,956 to clean up in 2019 compared to $131,549 just three years earlier. Graffiti-related arrests are down while incidents are up.

The subways aren't 100 percent littered with graffiti just yet, but crime has returned to them. Even during a time period in April where ridership averaged 9 percent of what it was pre-pandemic, felonies committed on the subway spiked 35 percent, largely driven by a rise in robberies. That coincides with an 87 percent decline in arrests on the subway (from 955 to only 124),

---

227 "AOC Calls $1B NYPD Budget Cut Insufficient: 'Defunding the Police Means Defunding the Police,'" Causes.com, July 7, 2020. https://www.countable.us/articles/45348-aoc-calls-1b-nypd-budget-cut-insufficient-defunding-police-means-defunding-police.

while summonses issued crashed from thirteen thousand to three hundred.[228]

That aside, de Blasio does care when graffiti happens to government buildings, but not private property. Speaking at a press briefing, de Blasio was asked about why graffiti was being removed on City Hall but not the buildings surrounding it. "Graffiti on public buildings will be removed, period. We've been dealing with budget challenges. We can't do everything that we used to do in terms of private buildings," de Blasio said.[229]

De Blasio is pretending that there's no money to clean up graffiti on everyone else's property. One of his spokespeople said that the program was suspended to "ensure the City can continue to devote resources to essential safety, health, shelter, and food security needs."

Graffiti-Free NYC's budget is $3 million,[230] out of an $86 billion budget. This would be the equivalent of an individual with a $100,000 annual budget cutting $3.49 in spending.

While $5 billion was slashed from the 2021 budget due to the pandemic, the City Council did make sure to include over $4 million in services for prostitutes, which will pay for their housing, medical care, job training, legal services, and street

---

228 Craig McCarthy, David Meyer, Julia Marsh, and Aaron Feis, "Crime Up, Arrests Down on Subways Despite Record-Low Ridership," *New York Post*, April 29, 2020, https://nypost.com/2020/04/29/crime-up-arrests-down-on-nyc-subways-despite-low-ridership/.

229 "Graffiti Is Making a Big Comeback In NYC, but There's No Money in the Budget to Fight It," CBS New York, July 21, 2020, https://newyork.cbslocal.com/2020/07/21/graffitis-making-a-big-comeback-in-nyc-but-theres-no-money-in-the-budget-to-fight-it/.

230 Christian Murray, "Mayor Ends Popular Graffiti-Removal Program, Cites Budget Constraints," *LicPost*, July 21, 2020, https://licpost.com/mayor-ends-popular-graffiti-removal-program-cites-budget-constraints.

outreach. The "money for prostitutes" program began disbursing funds in 2019.[231]

Fare evasion is up, costing the city nearly $300 million in 2019, up over 50 percent from $189 million the year before.[232]

Alongside the return of those broken windows is the return of the iconic squeegee men. Their return was alarming enough to prompt the *New York Post*'s editorial board to draw attention to it:

> Absent urgent action, Gotham is headed rapidly back to the bad old days.
>
> This weekend, those pernicious squeegee men of the pre–Rudy Giuliani era were back in force, harassing drivers. In the old days, nothing better symbolized the loss of civility and law and order than guys with dirty rags swabbing windshields without permission—and demanding money for it.
>
> All this, of course, is to be expected in a city where low-level crimes are no longer considered crimes—and cops, as The Post reported, aren't even bothering to hand out summonses.

As a John Jay College report found, summonses for infractions such as public urination and open [alcohol] containers are down 48 percent since they were decriminalized in 2017. That is, law-breakers are at little risk of arrest or fines. Even many

231 Sara Dorn, "NYC Council to Pay $4M in Services for Sex Workers Despite Budget Cut," *New York Post*, August 8, 2020, https://nypost.com/2020/08/08/nyc-council-to-pay-4m-in-services-for-sex-workers-despite-cuts/.

232 Nicole Gelinas, "A Better Way to Fight New York's Fare-Beating Problem," *New York Post*, December 1, 2019, https://nypost.com/2019/12/01/a-better-way-to-fight-new-yorks-fare-beating-problem/.

offenses still considered criminal won't get you locked up. So what do miscreants have to fear?[233]

During the pandemic, the city decided to release the homeless from shelters to lower their risk of contracting the coronavirus and instead house them in hotels.[234] In all, about 20 percent of all NYC hotels are housing homeless people. Good luck trying to figure out the logic behind that.

The problems resulting from this policy are quite predictable; the homeless have spilled out onto the streets during the day. In the Upper West Side, three hotels housed hundreds of homeless men, who have turned the surrounding area "into a spectacle of public urination, catcalling, and open drug use." Among the homeless are the mentally ill, drug addicts, and registered sex offenders.[235] In one hotel, two sex offenders are staying one block from a playground.

Elsewhere, restaurants haven't been able to utilize outdoor dining because the homeless have deterred people from sitting there. One business owner in Long Island City said the homeless have simply sat down at the tables themselves and refused to leave.

---

233 *Post* Editorial Board, "With Squeegee Men Back, NYC's Bad Old Days Can't Be Far Behind," *New York Post*, February 18, 2020, https://nypost.com/2020/02/18/with-squeegee-men-back-nycs-bad-old-days-cant-be-far-behind/.

234 Courtney Gross, "Exclusive: Close to 20 Percent of NYC Hotels Are Housing the Homeless," Spectrum News NY 1, June 25, 2020, https://www.ny1.com/nyc/all-boroughs/homelessness/2020/06/25/close-to-20-percent-of-nyc-hotels-are-housing-the-homeless.

235 Jennifer Gould, Jason Beeferman, Tamar Lapin, and Laura Italiano, "Hundreds of New Homeless Turn UWS into a Spectacle of Drugs and Harassment: Residents," *New York Post*, August 6, 2020, https://nypost.com/2020/08/06/hundreds-of-new-homeless-bring-drugs-loitering-harassment-to-uws/.

Another entrepreneur who owns a sandwich shop found even his takeout service suffered because of the increasing lawlessness. "The people that live in this area, they don't want to come get food here. They're scared. If they come, then a homeless person follows them in asking for money, asking for a sandwich. Who wants to deal with that?"[236]

So bad is the problem that even one homeless man put into a hotel agrees with them. "Who wants craziness in front of your doorstep?" he said to a reporter.[237]

A number of makeshift homeless encampments have also sprung up around the city. An encampment of twenty homeless sprang up on a Chelsea street corner, blocking entrances to businesses and further deterring people from frequenting them with their presence.[238] One *New York Post* reporter who visited the encampment saw one person smoking crack, and another vagrant said a number of them use drugs.

Overall, homelessness is up 40 percent from 2012–2019.[239]

---

236 Larry Celona, Julia Marsh, and Bruce Golding, "Outdoor Seating Impossible for Some Eateries Thanks to Wild NYC Streets," *New York Post*, July 24, 2020, https://nypost.com/2020/07/24/eateries-cant-do-outdoor-seating-thanks-to-wild-nyc-streets/.

237 Lorena Mongelli and Lia Eustachewich, "NYC Homeless Man Says He 'Agrees' with Homeless Hotel Concerns," *New York Post*, August 14, 2020, https://nypost.com/2020/08/14/nyc-homeless-man-says-he-agrees-with-homeless-hotel-concerns/.

238 Georgett Roberts and Aaron Feis, "Chelsea Homeless Camp Thrives Despite de Blasio Vowing Action," *New York Post*, August 12, 2020, https://nypost.com/2020/08/12/chelsea-homeless-camp-thriving-despite-de-blasios-vow-of-action/.

239 Zach Williams, "Is de Blasio Passing the Buck on Street Homelessness?" *City & State New York*, December 18, 2019, https://www.cityandstateny.com/articles/policy/housing/de-blasio-passing-buck-street-homelessness.html.

And as the problems of the Dinkins era have returned, so have those combating it. Graffiti is on the rise, the squeegee men are back, violent crime is rising, and while prostitutes aren't crowding 42nd Street, they are subsidized by the city. The Guardian Angels began patrolling Central Park once again in 2015 for the first time since 1994, and saw a surge in membership after the George Floyd riots.[240]

Seldom one to speak out on current events, former New York Governor George Pataki warned in mid-July that New York City is on the verge of "regression to those dark days when criminals ruled the streets."

"When I took office, New York was the most dangerous state in America. People got used to safety over the last 20 years," he said during a radio interview.

"They don't remember the time back when we were so dangerous," he continued. "When parents were afraid to send their kids to school. And when tourists knew better than to come to New York. I'm worried about the future of New York."

Citing bail reform, he added, "In a short period of time, the radicals have taken over. Name one politician in the State of New York or the City of New York that's standing up and defending our police."[241]

---

240 Teny Sahakian, "Guardian Angels See Surge of New Members as Homeless Population Wreaks Havoc on Upper West Side," Fox News, August 17, 2020, https://www.foxnews.com/media/guardian-angels-see-a-surge-of-new-members-as-new-yorkers-are-left-to-their-own-devices.

241 Vincent Barone, "Former Gov. Pataki: NYC Seeing 'Regression to Those Dark Days' of Crime," New York Post, July 26, 2020, https://nypost.com/2020/07/26/former-gov-pataki-nyc-seeing-regression-to-those-dark-days-of-crime/.

While Giuliani has some obvious bias here, he also knows exactly what the conditions were before he took office, and observed the same patterns. "Within a few short months, the city that's been the safest large city in America for 20 years under me and Bloomberg is now becoming maybe the second or third most dangerous city after Chicago," he told Fox News less than a month after Pataki's comments.

"I have no doubt I could reduce the emergency," Giuliani said. "And in about six months I could have the crime declines going in exactly the right direction again. Except you just wouldn't have to pay attention, which I wouldn't, to Black Lives Matter, Al Sharpton and all these racial hucksters."

Of the police's relationship with de Blasio he added, "They hate him. They despise him. They feel that he's going to turn on them at every opportunity that he gets in order to satisfy Black Lives Matter or some other radical anti-American hate group."[242]

So close are the parallels to the Dinkins days that even the *New York Post*'s "Do Something" headline has a parallel. "We Need Someone to Run for Mayor Who Will Save New York" the *Post*'s headline reads from an article written by the editorial board.[243]

Anyone but de Blasio will do.

---

242 Teny Sahakian, "Rudy Giuliani Blasts de Blasio's Handling of New York City's Rise in Violent Crime," Fox News, August 10, 2020, https://www.foxnews.com/media/rudy-giuliani-on-how-he-would-solve-crime-in-nyc.

243 *Post* Editorial Board, "We Need Someone to Run for Mayor Who Will Save New York," *New York Post*, August 16, 2020, https://nypost.com/2020/08/16/we-need-someone-to-run-for-mayor-who-will-save-new-york/.

ABOUT THE AUTHOR

Matt Palumbo is *The Dan Bongino Show*'s "resident fact checker" and author of *The Conscience of a Young Conservative*, *In Defense of Classical Liberalism*, *A Paradoxical Alliance*, *Spygate*, and *Debunk This!*.